Classical Music in a Changing World

Crisis and Vital Signs

Edited by

Lawrence Kramer

Fordham University

and

Alberto Nones

Conservatory of Music of Gallarate;
Associazione Europea di Musica e Comunicazione (AEMC), Italy

Series in Music

VERNON PRESS

www.vernonpress.com

In the Americas:	In the rest of the world:
Vernon Press	Vernon Press
1000 N West Street, Suite 1200	C/Sancti Espiritu 17,
Wilmington, Delaware, 19801	Malaga, 29006
United States	Spain

Series in Music

Library of Congress Control Number: 2021931332

ISBN: 978-1-64889-377-3

Also available:

978-1-64889-151-9 [Hardback]; 978-1-64889-213-4 [Hardback, Audio CD Edition];

978-1-64889-273-8 [PDF, E-Book]

The audio tracks can be downloaded here: https://vernonpress.com/book/1281

Cover design by Vernon Press using elements designed by Freepik.

Contents

Foreword

Alberto Nones

AEMC and "G. Puccini" Conservatory of Music of Gallarate

This volume is the result of the third AEMC Conference on Music, Communication, and Performance, organized by the Associazione Europea di Musica e Comunicazione (AEMC) and held online—due to the COVID-19 pandemic—on June 27–28, 2020. The conference centered on the question "Is Classical Music Dead? Kramer's Inquiry Revisited." The contributions in the book examine this subject from a variety of angles. Each of them presents original research while also encouraging new thinking and debate on classical music today. We take "classical music" here to mean art music (not merely commercial or functional music) produced or rooted in the traditions of Western culture. Some chapters refer to the narrower definition of the crucial span from 1750–1820, while others imply a more general definition that can be applied to music that precedes and follows that period. The general premise is that this music has been, and will continue to be, an active force in history and society.

The pandemic and associated lockdowns have had a massive impact on musical performance, music teaching (especially instrumental and vocal lessons), and many other fields of musical activity. The Metropolitan Opera in New York is just one example of a musical institution announcing drastic measures, with all its activities canceled until the 2021–2022 season. The Teatro alla Scala in Milan, on the contrary, resumed its activity before Italy's second wave of lockdown measures, opening its doors to audiences of maximum 600 people—well below the hall's capacity of 2000. At the opening concert (featuring Richard Strauss's *Vier Letzte Lieder* and *Ein Heldenleben*, broadcast by RaiRadio3 for the Euroradio circuit), on September 29, 2020, conductor Zubin Mehta addressed the Italian institutions and public with these words (in Italian):

> Congratulations, not only to La Scala, but to Italy. Everywhere, Italy starts making music again. I have given seven concerts in Florence already in June. Why am I saying this? Because in America, throughout America, music is closed: the Metropolitan has ceased the whole season, the Los Angeles Opera too, likewise the Los Angeles Philharmonic, the New York Philharmonic, all closed. A tragedy, really. I don't criticize them; they have their reasons. But music is important. I went to the

ballet the day before yesterday [in Milan, in a break between the Maestro's own rehearsals], to feel the enthusiasm of the public. I felt it: the audience shows incredible joy … It made me very happy (Zubin Mehta, interviewed on September 28, 2020 by Gaia Varon for RaiRadio3, my tr.).

Actually, many artists—especially outside the circuits in which Mehta operates—were, during those same days, lamenting the neglect of artistic performance in Italy, where the first general lockdown had been very strict, and where the revival of activities in all fields was subject to rigorous rules and limitations. In any case, soon after Mehta's declarations, theaters closed again as the State had to try to gain control of a new rise of contagion. My position is that this pandemic has made our priorities explicit, with health and safety set above all the rest, including not only culture and leisure, but even work and economic growth. The challenge, it seems to me, is to strike a balance between the many, extremely delicate issues at stake.

I was giving, at the Conservatory of Music of Gallarate, a course on the history and historiography of music that focused on the philosophy of music, and hence the significance of music, in the nineteenth and twentieth centuries, a course that was proceeding peacefully when, on February 24, 2020, at the news of the first case of coronavirus in Italy, it was abruptly suspended alongside all other activities at Italian schools and universities. Gallarate is near Milan, in Lombardy, at the epicenter of the pandemic in Italy and Europe at that time. I resumed my courses via online teaching soon after, on March 9, one of the first to experiment that modality of teaching in my music institution. Continuing to discuss the relevance of classical music during a dramatic time of great hardship for so many, and seeing the interest and passion for music enduring and even growing in the students, was an experience I will not forget. The commitment of those students is to me the strongest sign of the vitality and importance of music in our lives.[1]

When Nietzsche said that without music, life would be an error, he necessarily had live music in mind. There was no real alternative at the time. Our own comfort with sound recording—something that Theodor Adorno, for one, relentlessly criticized—combined with the economics of the music

---

[1] I wish to mention here my students of that course, and especially two of them: guitarist Nicholas Nebuloni, whom I also invited to present at the online conference a video performance he produced as one of the assignments ("Equinox" by Toru Takemitsu, filmed outdoors at a venue featuring an artistic work by Giò Pomodoro dedicated to the summer solstice); and pianist Andrea Rocchi, who lost his father to COVID-19 on March 29, 2020.

industry, has encouraged us to forget just how essential live music remains to our sense of what music is and of what performance in the flesh contributes to our sense of life. We are urged to rethink what music is in our times, in our lives, and see what experience of music we want to make and offer others. We should reconsider what it means for music as an art form to be vital, be it music of the past or music of the present. And we should reflect on, and act upon, its social function, its importance for human enrichment, its contribution to making us who we are.

If the question of the viability of classical music needed to be asked once again during the pandemic, this book and the conference from which it originated are some of the outcomes. All the contributions that appear here have to do with the questions posed above.[2] They have been listed in an order that moves from the particular (a social context), to the general (more theoretical), and returns to the particular before the concluding essay. This order reflects a premise: that we are people situated in time and context, who from that context go on to confront ever bigger issues while remaining in a web of social relationships.

Chapter 1 approaches the question of the state of classical music, offering an answer by examining the past 100 years in Turkey. Özgecan Karadağlı first provides a brief history of the function of classical music in the late Ottoman Empire. She then relates it to the early Turkish Republic and its internal and external motivations for adapting Western art music with Turkish folk idioms in the creation of a national music. Using Ahmet Adnan Saygun as example, Karadağlı argues that classical music managed to break down barriers in the past, and arguably continues to do so. The chapter closes by showing how two recent classical concerts in Turkey offer evidence of reciprocal engagements between classical music, people, politics, and power. In Turkey, then, classical music is far from dead.

Chapter 2 explores the extent to which the question of classical music's relevance to society is dependent on the society we are talking about. Francisco Castillo examines the case of Colombia, but also references other countries in his discussion. As in other places, musical activity in Colombia involves a tension between traditional music and Western classical music. Although many musicological positions have tried to ease this tension—Castillo contends—the dominant narrative keeps offering Colombian musicians a binary choice: to either accept European cultural domination, and thereby abandon the connection with one's own national identity, or to reject classical music and contribute to the construction of a national identity. This situation

---

[2] I acknowledge content taken from abstracts provided to me by the authors.

has not meant the death of classical music—Castillo continues—but has led music education in Colombia to take a defensive position and portray classical music as a threat to local culture. Castillo's chapter diagnoses this polarization between "our" music and the music of "others," and discusses the inaccuracy of the associated dichotomies. The author highlights some of the problems involved in situating classical music as a threat to national values, and proposes new conceptual routes to approach the delicate balance between homogenization under dominant music and extreme relativism.

Chapter 3 also points to a specific place in a specific time, here through the cultural lens of cinema. Hamish Robb analyzes the role of music in Barry Jenkins's 2016 film *Moonlight.* In the film—Robb maintains—meaning is fostered in large part through composer Nicholas Britell's original classical music score. The film's primary motifs, identified by Robb as ocean and moonlight, express what he calls notions of cyclicity and fluidity, which in turn nurture the film's two main themes: the cycle of intergenerational destiny, and the fluid, slippery nature of vulnerability and identity. Robb shows how the articulation, dramatization, and internalization of these themes rely largely on the qualities and approaches associated with the classical music tradition, and argues that the composer creates interstitial sonic spaces for the types of interpretative possibilities that classical music affords. The chapter has an interesting footnote about the use of popular music in the film score, while asserting in the text that the classical music on the soundtrack plays a larger role. This points to the possibly different kinds of cultural work demanded from the different musical genres, a question to which I will turn again at the end of this introduction. As illustrated by the film that Robb examines, the vitality of classical music comes in part from the kind of work it is equipped to do.

Chapter 4 brings us to music theater. Discussing the relevance of contemporary music theater in the frame of classical music's role in society, Federica Marsico claims that music can and should (but has often struggled to) broaden the horizons of experience by breaking with comfortable social norms. Marsico's chapter focuses on Sylvano Bussotti, who stood out for his provocative breaking of sexual taboos and for his explicit representation of homoeroticism and diverse gender identities. Through a review of some of Bussotti's works, Marsico highlights the subversive power of music theater, arguing that classical music can relate experiences of marginalization and challenge discriminatory prejudices.

Chapter 5 orients the discourse toward a broader response to the conference's question. Natalie Tsaldarakis begins with two remarks: first, 2020 was Beethoven's 250th anniversary, widely observed despite most of the scheduled events being canceled; and second, the musicologist Daniel Leech-Wilkinson has asserted through social media that "classical music performance has nothing to say about current concerns" ("current concerns" remaining in need of a more precise contextualization, of course). Tsaldarakis tackles claims that classical music is insular and irrelevant by also considering two of Lawrence Kramer's writings that present musical works as a mirror of/for its audiences.

In Chapter 6, we close the circle by returning to the discourse on social context. Amy Damron Kyle discusses how classical music has suffered from contradictions and limitations grounded in gender. Kyle takes this now-familiar observation in new directions. She suggests that looking at the past may offer us historical reasons for our disappearing classical music culture today. Because we owe our definition of what classical music is and isn't largely to a musical canon formed in the late nineteenth century—Kyle maintains—classical music is not seen today as a living and changing art form. School curricula, instrument method books, music education, and even concert program notes often replicate the male-centered canon developed in a distant past. Yet classical music may itself offer a recognition of the biased philosophy surrounding the musical canon and inspire a quest for a broader context of music's rich and diverse history. Opening a conversation through the notion of collaboration between known (male) geniuses and barely known (female) ones may indeed be one of the possible ways to revitalize classical music.

The last chapter features an essay by Lawrence Kramer, who most notably set the question of the relevance of classical music a few years ago (Kramer, 2007). In the context of the events that recently pushed classical music—together with most other forms of music—into a corner, Kramer rebounds with a compelling provocation: taken for granted, at this point, that classical music is not the culturally authoritative form of music, but one niche addressed to a certain audience, the question to ask ourselves is not whether classical music rises or falls, but what it is, and thus what we need to affirm if we continue to value it. I leave the discussion of what classical music is in Kramer's perspective to the reading of his essay. I wish to stress here, however, a critical recommendation: in order to offer people the kind of classical music we imagine they will value, we must not entrench ourselves in a fortress, but open the windows and search for new audiences.

On this final point, a few last thoughts. It is generally agreed in the volume that the music can, or even should, be peeled away from the obsolescent cultural apparatus on which much of it still depends, either unthinkingly or for economic reasons, and that when it ceases to represent the modern-day version of the *ancien régime* its appeal to listeners is revitalized. Its rapprochement with popular culture, which was part of the argument in Kramer (2007) and is reflected here for instance in Robb's chapter, may be part of that story. One might say that the book indeed highlights music's capacity to travel outside its usual venues (hence Turkey and Colombia, respectively in

Karadağlı's and Castillo's chapters), and at the same time reveals how classical music culture can be reinvigorated in those venues in order to meet the needs of the present (women composers, LGBTQ composers, respectively in Kyle's and Marsico's chapters), and it shows how that can be done.

I should stress, however, that highlighting classical music's relevance in/to popular culture is not the only way forward. With some of the musical festivals I have directed, I too have experimented with placing classical music in settings other than concert halls—such as at dawns and sunsets in the mountains and riverbanks—trying (and often succeeding) to engage new audiences more accustomed to pop concerts, also thanks to programs that included crowd favorites or compositions endowed with popular resonances. But I've always also noted that something special happens when classical music is performed in traditional concert halls, supported by the kinds of rites that belong to them: the concentration, the silent waiting, the composure, the demands on the listener in terms of length, and complexity of the pieces performed—all of which still make classical music special. Classical music can be proud of its difference, in this sense. And this is a remark that most of us, and certainly the author of the last essay, may agree with.

The book is accompanied by a CD of some of the music presented and discussed at the conference,[3] with short notes on each of the tracks. Some of this music too may be seen as presenting instances of the possible interplay with "pop culture" introduced above. On the one end of the spectrum, we have pieces like Kopecký's *Ritorni,* which testifies, to me at least, the typical pride of a contemporary classical music that stubbornly goes its own way, without appealing to the taste of a general public formed elsewhere. And I can acknowledge that this piece, performed live by the same Trio Aperto in a concert hall within one of the festivals I direct (it was the last concert I organized in Porto Recanati, Italy, in February 2020, before the lockdown), impressed the audience in its own right—maybe also because it was balanced within a program including eighteenth-century compositions, which is of course another tried-and-true approach to programming. Included in the CD is also the world premiere of the latest string quartet by Lawrence Kramer himself, a piece that reminds me of a somewhat similar alliance between classical forms, modern languages, and freedom of imagination that is at play

---

[3] The audio (and video) recording of Lawrence Kramer's quartet by Eurasia Quartet, produced at the Kerani Music Studio in the Netherlands in June 2020, has been fully sponsored by the AEMC from an idea of mine as part of the first prize awarded to the quartet at the second AEMC International Chamber Music Competition. The other recordings, with the exception of Animo's, are home recordings / live performances primarily intended for presentation at the conference.

in Schoenberg's Fourth Quartet Op. 37 (a work put in dialog by Schoenberg, in turn, with Beethoven's Op. 132).[4] Another piece I wish to highlight is Lukas Piel's "The Journey of Alan Kurdi," which likewise received its online premiere at the third AEMC conference. This may arguably be seen as an example of contemporary classical music that somehow winks to pop music (and film music). But it is a most positive example of such an interplay, still presenting structure, demands on the performers, and artistic unity, as well as a profound involvement with history and society. Indeed, the composition, as the title suggests, evokes the picture of the body of a 3-year-old Syrian boy on a shore, which raised a wave of emotion throughout the world in 2015, before the sea returned to stillness. Is classical music dead? My impression is that it is not. Despite 2020.[5]

References

Adorno, T. W. 2004 [1949]. *Philosophy of Modern Music*. Translated by A.G. Mitchell and W. V. Blomster. London and New York: Continuum.

Kramer, L. 2007. *Why Classical Music Still Matters*. Berkeley and Los Angeles: University of California Press.

Mehta, Z. 2020. "Interview with Gaia Varon for RaiRadio3 of September 28, 2020." https://www.raiplayradio.it/programmi/radio3suite-ilcartellone/arc hivio/puntate/. Accessed September 30, 2020.

Restagno, E. 2014. *Schönberg e Stravinsky. Storia di un'impossibile amicizia*. Milano: Il Saggiatore.

---

[4] This dialog between Schoenberg and Beethoven, recalled by Enzo Restagno (2014: 276), was shown in 1937 at the Royce Hall of the University of Los Angeles, where the composer programmed his four Quartets within a four-day concert in which they were performed, respectively, next to Beethoven's Op. 127, Op. 130-133, Op. 131, and Op. 132, thereby aiming to show a continuity. Interestingly, Restagno notes how an "art of memory" (2014: 278) features in the utilization of the material in Schönberg's Fourth Quartet, which is something that echoes in both Kramer's Quartet (starting from the very subtitle, *Reflections and Memories*), and in the argument that Kramer makes about the centrality of memory in classical music in Chapter 7, through his example of Schubert's Op. 100.

[5] A big thanks to my friend Alessandro Stella, who helped me compile the audio files that appear in the attached CD; Hamish Robb, who proofread the text and assisted me in other steps of the editorial process; and Larry Kramer, who first accepted my invitation to give the keynote at the third AEMC conference, and then embraced my proposal to co-edit this work with me, contributing a great deal to the coming into existence of this book as it is. Thanks also to Ellisa Anslow and Argiris Legatos of Vernon Press for their continued support, and to Gabrielle Curran for creating the Index and a consistent text, in terms of punctuation and formatting, from a diversity of contributors.

Chapter 1

The state of classical music: a Turkish detour

Özgecan Karadağlı

University of Alberta

Abstract

Addressing the question of the state of classical music and offering an answer by examining the past one hundred years in Turkey, the paper first provides a brief history of the function of classical music in the late Ottoman Empire. It then turns to the early Turkish Republic to discuss the internal and external motivations for adapting Western art music with Turkish folk idioms to create a national music. Using Ahmet Adnan Saygun as an example, the paper argues that classical music managed to break down barriers in the past and arguably continues to do so. The paper closes by showing how two recent classical concerts in Turkey offer evidence of reciprocal engagements between classical music, people, politics, and power.

Keywords: Western art music, Turkish folk music, Turkification, nationalism, Ahmet Adnan Saygun

* * *

When someone states or even implies that classical music is dying or dead, I am tempted to respond in a similar fashion to American humorist Mark Twain's legendary quip upon hearing of his own death: "The reports of my death are greatly exaggerated." Do they mean that no one is writing, performing, or listening to it? Or do they mean fewer people are buying and listening to it? Is the question even nullified in the asking? Unlike a person's, a music genre's death is difficult to quantify. And perhaps the question is not one to be answered by us—meaning the academic practitioners, purveyors, and performers. Rather, the answer(s) might more meaningfully lie in the creation and performance of classical music, and its embrace or dismissal by people, politics, and power. This answer is, to some degree, more assessable, and requires us to look beyond our own current place and time.

To offer an answer from a perhaps unusual perspective, the place and time I will look at are the first decades of the Turkish Republic, a place and land that had experienced "transculturation" (Ortiz, 1947), and thus an identity crisis, several times. There is a conventional Orientalist image of Turkey that often creates critical blind spots because of Western ideological leanings. But what does that have to do with classical music?

The tension of hundreds of years of an East-West dichotomy is sometimes, though not always, eased through art and music. Somehow via art/music we find a way to lessen the perceived otherness. In his novel *My Name Is Red*, the Turkish Nobel Prize-winning writer Orhan Pamuk tells an intercultural tale set in the days of the Ottoman Empire; a story about the conflict between the Western and Eastern approaches to painting—the portrait vs. miniature (Pamuk, 2002). The novel depicts an Imperial painter of miniatures who kills another painter to protect the traditional way of representation. He acts on the fear that the tradition, and maybe eventually even the people, would be changed by Western art. His violence is born of nostalgia in reverse, a sadness for a tradition he feared he would lose.

At the time of Pamuk's tale, another art form, Western art music, was already being introduced to the Empire, but instead of facing such a fearful response, eventually ripened and was enjoyed by the general public. The subsequent development of Western art music during the late Ottoman Empire and the early Turkish Republic does not have a well-documented history. Nonetheless, it offers a rich narrative because it proved possible to construct the mental representation of the nation through music. Western art music was introduced principally as a part of a reform movement in the military, and it progressed in the Empire predominantly through the work of Italians, particularly after Giuseppe Donizetti's arrival in Constantinople in 1828 under the title of "Colonel and Head Master" of the Imperial Bands. The fondness for Western music was so strong at the turn of the century that the Ottomans were debating whether to adopt Beethoven's Turkish March from *The Ruins of Athens*, Op. 113 as a national anthem (Araci, 2006: 96). Such a consideration aligned with the Ottomans' understanding of themselves as the successors to the Eastern Roman Empire. After the fall of Constantinople (1453), Mehmet the Conqueror claimed the title of Kayser-i Rûm (Cesar of the Romans), which, most likely for political reasons, was recognized by Greek philosopher George of Trebizond and the Eastern Orthodox Church (Crowley, 2005).

470 years later, during the second decade of the twentieth century, the Turkish nation-state was established based on the basis of various theories of nationalism, particularly the idea of an "imagined community" in which the

Turkish people (supposedly) shared the same values, language, and culture, and thus a new national identity (Anderson, 1983). Immediately after the proclamation of the new Republic, Mustafa Kemal Atatürk, the founder of modern Turkey, rapidly put into place sweeping cultural, educational, and social reforms that affected nearly all aspects of Turkish life. The policy makers did not see any contradiction in combining Turkification with Westernization because the combination was seen as almost equal to modernization, and the two policies were practiced simultaneously. During the construction of this new Turkish identity, Kültür Politikaları were recognized by the ideologs and by Atatürk himself as a necessary part of the transformation efforts. The cultural policies of Atatürk, according to Metin And, had two aspects: political-organizational and cultural-artistic aims (And, 1984: 218–22). The principles of the ideolog Ziya Gökalp strongly influenced Atatürk's ideological and aesthetic positions. Based on Gökalp's objectives, music, and other performing arts were used as a propaganda media, particularly through the network of Halkevleri (ibid)—a civil rights project intended to enlighten the citizenry and curb the influence of cultural conservatives. In this context, music became the focal point.

The fusion of Western music with Turkish folk idioms to create a national music had both internal and external motives. The internal goal was, as might be expected during the acculturation process, to consolidate the new aesthetic values of the Republic in order to create a culturally unified and cohesive nation-state. During this process, Turkish folk music, chosen for its symbolic power, was reconstructed to reflect the political aspects of Turkish nationalism and the formation of the nation-state (Tekelioğlu, 2001; Değirmenci, 2006; Öztürkmen, 1993; Stokes, 1992). Monogenesis theories of the folk tunes helped the policy makers not only to solidify the newly constructed folk (Halk), but also to create a cultural myth during the process of transculturation. These well-established musical idioms made it easy to focus on a (putatively) shared culture and to provide social continuity together with a well-defined identity.

The external goal of the adoption of Western music, one can argue, was the desire to change the centuries-long perception of the sonic image of Turkishness and Turkish music. Even though the Janissaries and their military band had been abolished in 1826 during a reform movement, Turkish music was persistently equated with the military band's sonic qualities, and for some, even until now, it still is. Turkishness was frequently and insistently associated with barbarism, cruelty, and bloodthirstiness because the West was threatened by the imperial goals of the Ottomans—a reversal of the painter's fear in Pamuk's story. Atatürk wanted to change the musical perception of the Westerners, and thus the clichéd perception of the Orient, and to eliminate some of the cultural barriers between Turkey and Europe. He was hoping to focus on shared auditory aesthetics, values, and ideals, and thus hopefully to diminish the East-West dichotomy.

These implementations, however, had multiple repercussions as the arts and music were institutionalized during the nationalizing process. There were two seemingly paradoxical consequences of the top-down policies. The first was to, knowingly or unknowingly, produce "otherness" and heighten awareness of ethnicity. In constructing Turkishness, the non-Turks are both being defined and defining themselves in opposition. They become "other." The cultural meanings of many kinds of music thus shifted toward an ideological narrowing. The second outcome was that the oral tradition was re-contextualized and folk music was standardized, largely as a result of efforts by the Turkish composer and ethnomusicologist Adnan Saygun and others, including Béla Bartók, to collect folk melodies and songs in Anatolia (Karadağlı, 2020). Although such folk music collections changed the very nature of the music, the melodies they contained enabled the conjunction of past and the present myths, and thus provided cultural identity and continuity. Through these melodies and the compositions that drew on them, the new republic's musical boundaries were set. The collections were treated as national treasures and used for didactic purposes, particularly by the first generation of composers, the Turkish Five.

Saygun, one of these composers, although classically trained in Europe, wrote music in which these idioms were meant to appeal to the newly constructed "folk" so that the "new music" became relevant to them because its idiom "belonged" to them. Unlike Adornian "experts," as Subotnik points out (1978: 744), the new experts, such as Saygun, sought to be accessible to the target audience they were trying to influence with the new idioms. One of Saygun's most important compositions, *Yunus Emre Oratorio* (1942), Op. 26, takes its name from and uses texts of the eponymous Anatolian mystic (c. 1240–1320). Although Chorale No. 5 is the only piece in the oratorio in which the original text and hymn melody are employed verbatim, Saygun capitalized on the centuries-long familiarity with Yunus Emre's mystical poetry—poetry that had been widely chanted in hymns in even the smallest villages in Anatolia. In using the familiar idiom in both melody and text, and while also pushing his audience to the less familiar, Saygun, one could surmise, was hoping to elevate the audience's level of sophistication and enable them to take in more abstract styles. In later pieces, such as *Aksak Sketches* (1976), Saygun's heavy use of thematic, rhythmic, and textural transformations requires a more trained ear to identify the traces of folk material.

Having digressed outside our time and place, let us return to the question of whether classical music is dead or still relevant today. In Turkey, it was through Saygun's and other Turkish composers' music, guidance, and teaching that classical music managed to break down the barriers of the "static core repertoire" (Kramer, 1995: 3) as the music meant more than music: it became the mental representation of the nation because of the meanings it accumulated from national history. But one can argue that almost a century later the meaning, reception, function, and the aesthetics have changed, and it is thus fair to ask if Saygun along with the classical music canons are still relevant in today's Turkey. The rhetorical and symbolic significance of classical music might have shifted; however, it is possible to talk about an unexpected classical music revival. The shift not only occurred in how classical music is perceived, but in who is listening and who is performing. The growing urban culture and audience, without a doubt, are responsible for the change in the perception and reception of classical music.

Even though Kerman argues that "repertoires are determined by performers, canons by critics" (Kerman, 1983), the perception of Saygun's music has recently been altered. Over the years, critics and academics have been critical of Saygun because of his early engagements with policy makers, resulting in some, such as Woodard (1999, 2007), finding his music one-dimensional in nature, and that dimension political. However, these critiques have been challenged by both Turkish and non-Turkish performers, the latter including YoYo Ma, Ari Rasilainen, and Joel Fan. It is almost as if the present generation has reclaimed the aesthetic value of Saygun's music, along with that of contemporary Turkish composers such as Hasan Uçarsu and Özkan Manav. In the last couple of decades, particularly, performers have been regularly including Saygun's pieces in their repertoires, signifying that Saygun's music has become part of the national canon and is perceived as cultural capital. Even in the midst of the current COVID-19 pandemic, performers from the younger generation in Turkey independently broadcast Saygun's performances, and Saygun's well-known former student, the pianist Gülsin Onay, has been interviewing weekly other former students about Saygun.

The performances, more than the interviews, reveal that the audience is growing and surprisingly getting younger—even including teenagers. This seemingly contradicts what may in fact be true in many places: that the audience for classical music is "shrinking, greying, and overly pale-faced" and that its institutions "squander its capacities for self-renewal by clinging to an exceptionally static core repertoire" (Kramer, 1995: 3–4). Classical music listeners in Turkey used to belong to the privileged classes; now, the new generation of performers and the listeners are mostly from middle and lower-middle-class families; some are even from practicing Muslim families. The entry exams of the state conservatories and the music faculties are unreasonably competitive, and sometimes children try for years to be accepted. Since even private universities' music departments offer full scholarships for successful students, the tuition is not an issue in most cases and the instruments are provided by the schools. Gender representation is also quite balanced, with conducting the only area still heavily male-oriented.

Even though most people are not music literates, classical music has been quite affordable for most classes through the state opera-ballets and the symphonic orchestras, music festivals, and radio broadcasts. Consequently, the criticism of classical music being elitist is being transformed; in the urban settings, listening to classical music is not necessarily a sign of class. During the last three decades, beyond the state orchestras, private corporations, and universities have established private orchestras because of the growing audience. All these dynamics have greatly contributed to the revival of classical music. One of the factors for secular Turks who listen to classical music and to Turkish composers is the meaning that has been attributed to the music, embracing a modern, secular nostalgia that signifies the symbolic Turkish renaissance of the twentieth-century Republic.

Two recent classical concerts held in Turkey highlight the foregoing and offer evidence of reciprocal engagement between classical music and people, politics, and power. In a January 2019 concert, the internationally acclaimed Turkish pianist and composer Fazıl Say, well-known for his strong opposition to Turkey's conservative government and its leader, had an unexpected guest in the audience: Turkish president Recep Tayyip Erdoğan. The symbolic significance of this incident was considerable. The president attended a classical concert with American Republican senator Lindsey Graham—a surprisingly similar political-music affair to one that Atatürk held during the visit of the Shah of Iran in 1934 (Karadağlı, 2017: 80). This turn of events was unanticipated as Say has been quite vocal about his opposition to Erdoğan, and classical music represents in its history and symbolism the substance of much that the President ideologically and religiously opposes. Erdoğan has openly criticized the founders of the Republic, and denounced classical music as an imposition by the Republic, even abolishing the traditional Republic Balls that started in 1925.

The second classical concert was held in the Presidential Palace in Ankara in July 2020, on the anniversary of the 2016 coup attempt. Every aspect of the concert was unexpected: the composer, Fahir Atakoğlu, known for his soundtracks of important documentaries on the recent history of the Republic, including one on Mustafa Kemal Atatürk; the concert venue; and, most importantly, the genre of music. No one would have predicted that President Erdoğan would host such an event with such music as generally he is ideologically opposed to the West(ern culture). Of course, the occasion was a well-calculated political strategy and a symbolic gesture: it either showed President Erdoğan trying to connect with his strong opposition and almost claiming a place from the "other neighborhood," the secularists' territory;

and/or, showed him following in the footsteps of the late Ottoman caliph Sultans, for whom he has great admiration, having the desire to revive the "mighty" Empire. One might even read the recent controversial move to change the status of the Hagia Sophia from a museum to a mosque as a sign to secularist Turks, more than to Westerns, of such a longing for a return to the Empire. The message seems to be to highlight and dismiss Atatürk's anti-imperialist attitude in the light of Turkey's latest political and military moves.

Historically, music has been a politicized entity in Turkey and has had significant sociocultural agency; currently, because of the ongoing polarization, music, particularly classical music, sometimes becomes the battlefield of this political clash. Sometimes a classical music concert can also be seen as a symbolic act of rebellion against political authority and its hegemonic power. The more the conservative government pushes their conservative/religious values, the more people use music as a political-aesthetic statement. Compared to Europe, classical music might still be in its infancy in Turkey; but in less than 200 years, classical music has become an irrevocable tradition, with a solid audience, performers, and supporting institutions. So even though the tradition is relatively new, the interest and the fondness are sincere. For the last 100 years, the role and the function of classical music ranged from achieving extensive socio-political goals to realizing aesthetically motivated values; and it functioned politically as a unifying agent between different classes of society. Thus, the motivation is not always necessarily musical, but sometimes aesthetic, sometimes political, and sometimes pedagogical. And it is this ever-changing multi-motivational dynamic, engaging people, politics, and power, that has the ability to reimagine, reinvigorate, and reinvent, if need be, art—in this case, classical music.

References

Anderson, B. 1983. *Imagined Communities: Reflections on the Origin and Spread of Nationalism*. London: Verso.

And, M. 1984. "Atatürk and the Arts with Special Reference to Music and Theater." In *Atatürk and the Modernization of Turkey*. Boulder, Colorado: Westview Press-Leiden: E.J. Brill: 215–233.

Aracı, E. 2006. *Donizetti Paşa Osmanlı Sarayının İtalyan Maestrosu.* Istanbul: Yapı Kredi Yayınları.

Crowley, R. 2005. *Constantinople: the last great siege, 1453*. London: Faber and Faber.

Değirmenci, K. 2006. "On the Pursuit of a Nation: The Construction of Folk and Folk Music in the Founding Decades of the Turkish Republic." *International Review of the Aesthetics and Sociology of Music* 37(1): 47–65.

Karadağlı, Ö. 2017. *From Empire to Republic: Western Art Music, Nationalism, and the Merging Mediation of Saygun's Op. 26 Yunus Emre Oratorio.* s.l.: s.n.

--------2020. "Bartok's Influence on Saygun: Collaboration and Transmutations." *Ethnomusicology Journal* 3(1): 56–76.

Kerman, J. 1983. "A Few Canonic Variations." *Critical Inquire* 10(1): 107–125.

Kramer, L. 1995. *Classical Music and Postmodern Knowledge.* Berkeley: University of California Press.

Ortiz, F. 1947. *Cuban Counterpoint: Tobacco and Sugar.* New York: A.A. Knopf.

Öztürkmen, A. 1993. *Folklore and Nationalism in Turkey.* s.l.: Unpublish PhD diss.

Pamuk, Orhan. 2002. *My Name is Red.* Trans. Erdag Göknar. New York: Vintage.

Stokes, M. 1992. *The Arabesk Debate.* Oxford: Clarendon Press.

Subotnik, R. R. 1978. "The Cultural Message of Musical Semiology: Some Thoughts on Music, Language, and Criticism since the Enlightenment." *Critical Inquiry* 4(4): 741–768.

Tekelioğlu, O. 2001. "Modernizing reforms and Turkish music in the 1930s." *Turkish Studies* 2(1): 93-108.

Woodard, K. 1999. *Creating a National Music in Turkey: The Solo Piano works of Ahmet Adnan Saygun.* s.l.: University of Cincinnati Unpublished DMus Thesis.

Woodard, K. 2007. "Music Mediating Politics in Turkey: The Case of Ahmed Adnan Saygun." *Comparative Studies of South Asia, Africa and the Middle East* 27(3): 442–462.

Chapter 2

Local music and the classical music of others: misconceptions and possibilities in Colombian musical education

Francisco Castillo

FJdC District University – ASAB Bogotá

Abstract

The paper explores whether classical music's relevance to society depends on the society we are talking about. It examines the case of Colombia, but also references other countries in the discussion. As in other places, musical activity in Colombia involves a tension between traditional music and Western classical music. Although many musicological positions have tried to ease this tension, the dominant narrative keeps offering Colombian musicians a binary choice: to either accept European cultural domination and thereby abandon the connection with one's own national identity, or to reject classical music and contribute to the construction of a national identity. This situation has not meant the death of classical music, but has led music education in Colombia to take a defensive position and portray classical music as a threat to local culture. The paper diagnoses this polarization between "our" music and the music of "others" and discusses the inaccuracy of the associated dichotomies, proposing new conceptual routes to approach the delicate balance between homogenization under dominant music and extreme relativism.

Keywords: otherness, Colombia, music education, identity

* * *

A few years ago, I conducted a research project on colonial music. I decided to present some of my progress at a conference on Colombian music organized by colleagues in Bogotá. My paper was rejected because it seemed to the committee that my study did not fit with the theme of the event. Generally, when any of my proposals for a conference or journal is rejected, I do what we all do: talk to friends and study more. However, this time I also felt that an interesting idea was opening for me: the committee considered that this music was not Colombian. It was categorized by them as "other" music.

Although many musicological positions have tried to ease this tension, the dominant narrative in Colombia continues to offer the nation's musicians a binary world according to which we must choose between two options: either to accept European cultural domination and thereby abandon the connection with our national identity, or to reject European classical music and contribute to the construction of (a) national identity. Given this situation, this paper has three main objectives: (1) to diagnose this division; (2) to break down the polarization between "our music" and "the music of others"; and (3) to discuss the inaccuracy of this dichotomy.

This paper is based on what happens inside ASAB, Academia Superior de Artes de Bogotá, the Arts Faculty of District University in Bogotá, the music education program of which has included both traditional and classical music studies. However, there are good reasons to think that behind this case can be read a broader phenomenon. The tension between local values and those associated with Europe are a frequent topic in many countries that were part of the colonialist project in America, Asia and Africa. In this context, it can be supposed that the vindication of national values has helped to imagine the death of classical music. As will be explained later, the antagonism that requires the death of one musical tradition to guarantee the existence of another is a product of fallacious reasoning. Recognition of this fallacy leads to the inference that classical music is not dead.

Diagnosis

I analyzed four types of documents: student projects, syllabi, institutional documents, and conferences. For the analysis of the documents, I have relied on critical reading, discourse analysis, and data mining tools.

The projects carried out by my students revealed the concepts absorbed during their pre-university education, many of which persist in organizing history according to teleological or evolutionary metaphors. As for the division between "us" and "others," the evidence suggests that the basic education system has fallen into the trap of oversimplifying discourses in order to simplify their students' understanding. It is easier to imagine a Latin American country as the territory where a fight between local and foreign values takes place than it is to understand the country in the full complexity of its history. By teaching children history as a story in elementary school, historical agents are shaped as "good guys" and "bad guys," and so students end up taking sides. The discovery of America has been presented under this model for a long time. While there are a significant number of historians who have helped to deconstruct these myths (Roca, 2016; Restall, 2004), their ideas have been relegated to narrow circles of historiographical reflection.

The binary attitude affects music instruction directly. While piano, violin, and cello syllabi emphasize what is expected from the student, the syllabi for traditional instruments emphasize the potential contribution to the cultural development of the region. This reinforces a narrative by which we are divided: some musicians work towards a national identity while others give continuity to classical tradition. While the viola syllabi reference canonical works organized under a standard typology, the syllabus for *bandola* highlights the absence of a standardized technique, and the one for the *charango* refuses to mention specific works, favoring genres or popular airs instead.

At the base of the ASAB's operation is the *Self-Assessment Report*. From its analysis, we can infer that the entire report points to plurality. The document follows the route outlined by anthropology (Geertz, 2003), according to which the expression "culture" in its singular form should not be used. Following this direction, the report makes constant use of expressions such as "musics" and musical arts, evidencing a political position grounded in a program of cultural relativism. But it should be noticed that each mention of musical traditions or practices is expressed in terms of an opposition between "Western academic music and local or regional musics from Colombia and Latin America." Note that the plural has not been used in a balanced way, as what is pluralized is "local musics" as opposed to "Western academic music," expressed as one.

Concerning academic conferences, the set of papers presented at the events organized by the ASAB reveals a concern about the ways in which traditional or popular music is integrated into the music education system (Castillo, 2018). In a panoramic view, the history of the conferences that we have organized has followed the same implicit narrative found in the assessment report. Music education started by copying the European model. Later, the canon of composers was made more flexible, mentioning Colombian composers who had studied in Europe. Afterwards, it included local composers who had not studied abroad. Subsequently, the Academy opened to music from oral traditions, and regional musical instruments were also integrated along this route. Finally, the last decade has been characterized by studying the ways of learning and assessment that conflict when traditional music appears in the classroom. Although the process has followed a healthy route for debate, it has also perpetuated the binary vision of one music facing another music.

Events organized outside the ASAB reveal a more belligerent tone. Protecting Colombian music is a common *leitmotiv* in the narrative that constructs classical music as a threat to be addressed. An example is the MAC 2020 (MAC stands for "Músicas Andinas Colombianas," an annual conference): *Musics in a State of Resistance.* Given that title, it is worth asking: what or whom are you resisting? The tone of the papers presented at the conference, as well as the conference's characterization of its thematic lines, allows us to observe how the division is established: the return to local music becomes a sign of generational, political, or ideological resistance. In this and other conferences, the lexicon seems to place the two musics on a battlefield. "Music on the edge, on the front line" and "music in danger of extinction" are some of the recurring tropes.

Discussion

The division between "our musics" and "others' music" seems to ignore the ideas proposed by cultural history and global history, which have deconstructed the binary narrative of victims and victimizers in favor of a careful revision attentive to syncretism and musical migration. The need to insist on classifying music in only one of two categories may have arisen from the appeal of cultural relativism. Because relativism is such an attractive position in countries that have been subject to unequal power relations, it is possible to suggest that by dividing music in this way we are also moving away from imperialist political positions that we reject for historical and ethical reasons.

Questions posed by authors such as Kofi Agawu are quite relevant. In his analysis of Africanist musicology, he discussed the extent to which scholars like Hornbostel thought about African music along the lines of something different from the music "we are used to." Agawu points out that "by constructing phenomena, objects, or people as 'different,' one stakes a claim to power over them" (Agawu, 2003). The contradiction is ironic, in that "othering" in order to denounce unbalanced relations of political power ends up becoming a form of exclusion itself that can also include aggressive forms of power. This irony is consistent with the findings of the conferences analyzed: multiculturalism is privileged as long as it excludes European culture.

Born (2000) points out that ideas from post-colonial studies and postmodernist theory operate underneath this division between Western (classical) music and other musics. Both fields have enjoyed wide acceptance in Latin American musicological circles. While the questions triggered by colonialism have been decisive to the arts and humanities, allowing our cultural identity to become a story of others—with their music as bad guys versus us, the good guys, with our musics—caricatures reality. Postmodernism also has its risks: Lyotard's skepticism of metanarratives can lead to completely disconnected stories (Gloag, 2015; Kramer, 1995). Perhaps, with the weapons provided by post-colonialism and postmodernity, Colombian music has become defensive. In Colombia, folk studies were in charge of this defense for many years. The strategy they used was to protect local traditions from Anglo-European homogenization, and they thought that the best way to protect a musical tradition was to isolate it and give it a name (Miñana, 2000). If local cultures safeguarded an essential part of national identity, many researchers understood the relation between local and European music as a constant struggle to remain pure from colonial influences.

On the other hand, all the documents I analyzed placed special emphasis on the importance of placing the musical phenomenon within its cultural context. Although this turn could constitute a response to ethnomusicology or to New Musicology, its contextualism in this case implies a critical and belligerent position. "Assuming that traditional music should be revitalized by its close connection with its context seems to oppose classical European music since in the past it was thought that classical music was superior precisely because it was immune to such undesirable social forces" (Shepherd, 2003). The idea of such immunity reflects the thinking of Schopenhauer or Hanslick much more than that of contemporary musicological discourse. When I call my students' attention to these issues, they often ask: "So then, is it all the same?" To answer this complex question, I have been trying to use the continuum approach in my own courses. Rather than being a model or a format, it is a way to disrupt the opposition between our music and that of others. This idea owes a lot to Hobsbawm (2012) and especially to Schippers (2009).

Other dichotomies (on a continuum)

Oral   ⟵⟶   Notated

Some types of music require little or no use of scores while other musical practices depend on them to a great extent. Obviously, there is a dose of orality in a Brahms symphony, and there are also different scores for *cumbia*, but Brahms and *cumbia* are not located in the same place in a continuous scheme.

Sometimes music itself can be mobilized along the continuum; sometimes a collective musical practice can offer different positions for different members. For example, in a band, a tenor saxophone may have to follow a score closely, while the trumpet knows that he/she must read some parts and improvise others, the guitar only has a few chords written down, and the drummer may be playing everything by ear. Thus, the practice would be very oral for some, very mediated by notation for others, and in gray zones for others, all simultaneously.

Body   ◀━━━━━━━━━━━━━━▶   Mind

Another fissure is the mind-body dichotomy. It is possible to attribute to classical music a tendency to make the body invisible in its discourses. Apart from pedagogical approaches of the last decades, classical music has conceived the body as an obstacle that prevents transit between ideas and results. Music where dance is indispensable, or where tapping the floor is cultivated and well-received, tends more to the left of the continuum.

Senses   ◀━━━━━━━━━━━━━━▶   Reason

As in the previous cases, it is difficult to sustain the thought that reason and the senses are separate domains. However, there are musical practices that privilege the logocentric theoretical exercise, and others in which words, measurements, and musical theory play a minor role.

Local   ◀━━━━━━━━━━━━━━▶   Universal

Much of European musical thought in past centuries was characterized by a universalizing of musical principles. The identification of certain composers as "great masters" or of music as a "universal language"—something that used to be very frequent, and to some extent still is—shows that European values were assumed to be universal, even over and above the strong influence of nationalism within Europe. Closer to the other end of the continuum, we can find musical manifestations that have no will to become universal: music that is recognized as local and which participates in a discourse of regional or national identity.

No-Work   ◀━━━━━━━━━━━━━━▶   Work

Collective re-appropriation characterizes traditional Colombian music. The indeterminate ontology of some musical practices can be opposed to a more concrete ontology, condensed sometimes under the concept of musical work. Beethoven's piano sonatas are good examples of closed works, lying closer to the right-hand side of the scheme. Traditional Latin American airs, open form, or indeterminate instrumentation tend more towards the left-hand side of the continuum.

Unknown   ◀━━━━━━━━━━━━━━▶   Canonic

Discussion of canonical composers and works is now commonplace in texts and spaces for historiographical reflection. When certain music is considered a fundamental part of a complete education, it approaches the right-hand side of the continuum. As in the previous cases, this division rather complicates the situation: thanks to their search for (a) national identity, some local composers have been canonized just as Bach or Mozart have been by other standards.

Rural   ⟵━━━━━━━━━━━━━━━⟶   Metropolitan

Finally, the geographic location of musical practices can help us characterize them as well, but in a multidirectional way. "Peasant music" is a common expression in Colombia. Although its lyrics usually mention peasant cultural practices, the use and dissemination of this music has found an enormous reception in big cities, where many traditional pieces of music find audiences, recording studios, etc. Music can move in the other direction too. "Alma Llanera," a song used that has a cultural icon in the plain lands of Venezuela and Colombia, began as a *zarzuela* in a theater, and then migrated to rural places. Somewhat similarly, compositions such as Viadana's *Officium Defunctorum*, performed today in venues typical of Western classical music, in 1616 might have had a more "peasant" sound, on account of its frequent use of extreme low-voice polyphony deriving from rural musical practice. For sure, what we include in classical music festivals was, in other times and in other places, anything but classical.

Conclusions

Characterizing musical practices according to dynamic continua (which are not binary or mutually exclusive) is far more complex than splitting music into two opposite containers labeled "ours" and "others." However, I think this is a healthy complexity insofar as it reflects the intricate problems of national identity. Using this approach enables one to form another perspective on the division between local and classical music. In the oral-score continuum, much traditional music leans to the left as do those who play *basso continuo* in baroque music and many contemporary music practices. On the local-universal continuum, the uses that have been made of Beethoven's Fifth are close to reggaeton or K-pop records, both having been subject to a huge dissemination around the world, so that people in Asia may find meaning in Beethoven, and Korean artists get to the top charts in Mexico and the USA. In Bohlman's words, "South American peoples also assemble 'our music' to distinguish it from 'theirs,' using practices of borrowing and bricolage not so vastly different from those of Jesuit missionaries in the so-called age of discovery" (Bohlman, 2001).

From this perspective, classical music is not dead, but its vitality is not derived from having resisted nationalism. Classical music is alive in the same way that the different factors that build our national identity are. If the simplistic model of *our* music and that of *others* is abandoned, killing classical music to favor our music makes no sense since we are made up of different types of music, classical and not-so-classical alike. In this context, giving vitality to classical music not only poses no threat to our cultural identity, but on the contrary forms a way of vitalizing it and looking at it from a more balanced position.

Whenever the Peasant Music Ensemble performs in a concert (Franco, 2018), it simultaneously mobilizes many of these continuums. The repertoire may include songs by well-known people from the genre who configure their own canon, but it may also include student compositions. Some students have learned the repertoire by ear, and others replicate the models as if from sheet music. Others improvise. Some dance with the music, but the public behaves as in a symphony concert. While many students come from the countryside, they learn these songs in the city and are awarded a numerical grade for their performance.

The assessment of these cases shows that the division between Colombian music and other classical music does not express all the internal gradations of the phenomenon. Now, considering that we are not the first to notice it, why does the divisive approach persist in our context?

This question deserves a deep and multidisciplinary examination, but my intuition suggests that one of the main factors is this: positioning oneself as a Colombian musician who promotes Colombian music endows subjects with a mission. Many of our social problems stem from dehumanizing capitalism, hegemonic politics, and violent homogenizations. Considering that the common narrative suggests that these problems come from outside, and that we as musicians want to participate in the solution, promoting our music is confused with protecting our social or cultural values from imperialism.

As suggested at the beginning, similar situations occur in places other than Latin America. Murtomäki (2015) discusses why Bohemian composers have been denied a place in musical historiography, and associates this denial with political phenomena such as German nationalism. Tokumaru (2018) wonders why, if music notation can be found in Japan prior to 747 and in printed scores from 1472, the study of Japanese music has been the province of ethnomusicology and not of historical musicology; he concludes that this disciplinary situation has been part of an othering unfavorable to Asian musicology. In post-independence India, both the state and popular music were sacralized, thereby reinforcing Hindu national identity, and at the same time gaining distance from colonial influence (Jones, 2013).

Although the literature on the tensions stemming from local musicologies is quite large, the sides of the debate are almost always the same. On one hand, "a demonized Other [is] necessary for the sake of self-definition" (Illari, 2013). On the other hand, Western musical style is used as a basis to construct a non-Western identity (Cook, 2013). For example, the exclusion of the *Kulag* (Korean traditional music) from Korean conservatories has been reversed only in recent decades, partly thanks to deep reflections on the Westernization of its principles and complex articulations with the North American model of music education that was imposed after liberation from Japan in 1945. Howard (2013) collects the relevant data, and from there asks highly provocative questions about the concepts and words used to describe musical practices: are "concerts" a European idea? Is "composition" a Western concept?

This fundamental challenge has been very well expressed by S. Conrad: "How can we overcome Eurocentrism and take account of the multiple positions from which history can be written without falling into the trap of nativism and without positing alternative forms of centrism?" (2017). The following question could be added to the discussion: how can we oppose classical music to other kinds without caricaturing it in a simple and pallid image? It should go without saying that imagining classical music as a unified tradition devoid of improvisation and orality and excluding the body and the senses is a simplification that not only ignores what we can know about the European musical past, but which can also be a kind of violence as radical as that which postmodernist and post-colonial thinking tends to attribute to modernity.

In a somewhat romantic but interesting solution, Harari (2018) proposes that nationalism was formerly a position asserting the failure of other nations in order to secure one's own national advantage. He adds that this position is no longer sustainable in the contemporary world. In social and economic terms, if the development of a foreign country can also benefit our nation, we could think that spreading Vivaldi's music in Colombia is no threat to national values, and that performing traditional music does not kill classical music.

Yet we must remain alert. Whenever any musical tradition is threatened with being homogenized or violently transformed, the possibility arises that human beings may be treated violently too. In such cases, the discussion about musical ontology and the debate around the composers' canon slide to the background, redirecting the utmost attention to the foreground as it undoubtedly concerns us all: that our music or the music of others—whether traditional or classical—take part in balanced, friendly, and peaceful human relationships.

References

Agawu, K. 2003. "Contesting Difference: A Critique of Africanist Ethnomusicology." In M. Clayton, T. Herbert and R. Middleton (eds.). *The Cultural Study of Music.* New York: Routledge: 226–237.

Bohlman, P. 2001. "Ontologies of Music." In N. Cook and M. Everist (eds.). *Rethinking Music.* New York: Oxford UP: 17–34.

Born, G. and D. Hesmondhalgh. 2000. *Western Music and Its Others. Difference, Representation, and Appropriation in Music.* Berkeley: University of California Press.

Castillo, F. 2018. "Introducción." In F. Castillo (ed.). *Encuentro sobre músicas populares y tradicionales en la educación musical.* [ebook] Bogotá: Facultad de Artes ASAB. Available at: http://fasab.udistrital.edu.co:8080/publica ciones. Accessed August 30, 2020.

Conrad, S. 2017. *Historia Global. Una nueva visión para el mundo actual.* Barcelona: Planeta.

Cook, N. 2013. "Western music as world music." In P. Bohlman (ed.). *The Cambridge History of World Music.* Cambridge: Cambridge University Press: 75–99.

Franco, E. 2018. "Crónica de un recorrido: el Ensamble de Músicas Campesinas del Proyecto Curricular de Artes Musicales de la Facultad de Artes ASAB de la Universidad Distrital Francisco José de Caldas." In F. Castillo (ed.). *Encuentro sobre músicas populares y tradicionales en la educación musical.* Bogotá: ASAB: 177–186.

Geertz, C. 2003. *La interpretación de las culturas.* 12th ed. Barcelona: Gedisa.

Gloag, K. 2015. "'A Thing of the Past': Canon Formation and the Postmodern Condition." In V. Kurkela and M. Mantere (eds.). *Critical Music Historiography: Probing Canons, Ideologies and Institutions.* New York: Routledge: 227–238.

Harari, Y. 2018. *21 lecciones para el siglo XXI.* Bogotá: Debate.

Hobsbawm, E. and T. Ranger. 2012. *The invention of tradition.* Berkeley: Cambridge University Press.

Howard, K. 2013. "Korean music before and after the West." In P. Bohlman (ed.). *The Cambridge History of World Music.* Cambridge: Cambridge University Press: 321–351.

Illari, B. 2013. "A story with(out) Gauchos: folk music in the building of the Argentine nation." In P. Bohlman (ed.). *The Cambridge History of World Music.* Cambridge: Cambridge University Press: 371–392.

Jones, J. 2013. "Music, history, and the sacred in South Asia." In P. Bohlman (ed.). *The Cambridge History of World Music.* Cambridge: Cambridge University Press: 202–222.

Kramer, L. 1995. *Classical Music and Postmodern Knowledge.* Berkeley: University of California Press.

Miñana, C. 2000. "Entre el folklore y la etnomusicología. 60 años de estudios sobre la música popular tradicional en Colombia." *A Contratiempo. Revista de música en la cultura* 11: 36–49.

Murtomäki, V. 2015. "Bohemian Composers Sidetracked in the Musical Historiography of 'Viennese Classicism.'" In V. Kurkela and M. Mantere (eds.).

Critical Music Historiography: Probing Canons, Ideologies and Institutions. New York: Routledge: 81–94.

Restall, M. 2004. *Los siete mitos de la conquista española.* Barcelona: Paidós.

Roca, M. 2016. *Imperiofobia y leyenda negra: Roma, Rusia, Estados Unidos y el Imperio español.* Madrid: Siruela.

Schippers, H. 2009. *Facing the music: Shaping music education from a global perspective.* New York: Oxford University Press.

Shepherd, J. 2003. "Music and Social Categories." In M. Clayton, T. Herbert and R. Middleton (eds.). *The Cultural Study of Music.* New York: Routledge: 68–78.

Tokumaru, Y. 2018. "Contemplating Musicology form Japanese Perspectives." *Musicological Brain Food* 2: 1–3.

Chapter 3

Waxing and waning: musical depictions of cyclicity and fluidity in *Moonlight*

Hamish Robb

Victoria University of Wellington, New Zealand

Abstract

The paper examines the role of music in Barry Jenkins's 2016 film, *Moonlight*, arguing that meaning in the film is fostered largely through composer Nicholas Britell's original, classical music score. The film's primary motifs, identified in the paper as ocean and moonlight, express notions of cyclicity and fluidity, which in turn nurture the film's two main themes: 1) the cycle of intergenerational destiny; and 2) the fluid, slippery nature of vulnerability and identity. The paper illustrates how the articulation, dramatization and internalization of these themes rely largely on the qualities and approaches associated with the classical music tradition. It argues that the composer creates interstitial sonic spaces for the types of interpretative possibilities that classical music affords.

Keywords: film music, classical music, Barry Jenkins, Nicholas Britell

* * *

In Barry Jenkins's 2016 film, *Moonlight*, meaning is fostered in large part through composer Nicholas Britell's original classical score. The film's primary motifs of ocean and moonlight express notions of cyclicity and fluidity, which in turn nurture the film's two main themes: 1) the cycle of intergenerational destiny; and 2) the fluid, slippery nature of vulnerability and identity. Importantly, the articulation, dramatization, and internalization of these themes rely largely on the original classical scoring, and on the qualities and approaches associated with the classical music tradition. In particular, the composer creates large, open spaces for the types of interpretative possibilities that classical music typically affords. Lawrence Kramer observes that in classical music, "the meanings that … become perceptible are not somehow contained in the music or simply revealed by it. They are made available to, and by, the listening subject, who must in part create them to experience them" (2007: 24–25). In *Moonlight*'s score, this rich participatory quality of classical music is augmented, not only through the trajectory of thematic transformations, but also through the establishment of musical "zones" outside of the typical boundaries of the musical "piece," and through the slowing down of the main theme to reveal more and more interstitial sonic spaces.

This chapter thus provides evidence of classical music's ability to furnish an exploratory sonic "space" within which meanings are formed, rather than merely found. Such spaces allow sound to enrich visual images, conceptual themes, and audience engagement in creative and profound ways. These exploratory possibilities, it will be seen, confirm classical music's continuing relevance, often in surprising contexts—in this film, within the gritty world of drugs, street survival, and hypermasculine swagger.

Moonlight's themes

Before examining the music of *Moonlight*, it is first necessary to understand the film's two central themes.

Theme 1—The cyclicity of intergenerational destiny

Depicting episodes from different periods of the central character's life, *Moonlight* is divided into three chapters that refer to the names the main character goes by at each stage: "Little" (as young boy), "Chiron" (as adolescent), and "Black" (as adult). The first part of the film presents Little growing up in a poor, drug-fueled neighborhood. Bullied by his classmates for being different, he must also endure the unpredictable moods of his mother, a drug addict. And from the opening scene, it is suggested that Little's future, too, will be marked by drugs. The camera circles around a corner dealer and a drug user in complete rotations, hinting at the cyclicity of fate that awaits Little. In the background, a man runs from the police, inviting us to recognize the harsh reality of these characters' lives. And immediately following, Little likewise runs through the scene; his entrance into the film mirrors the daily life of the drug user we have just observed. It is from school bullies that Little runs. And it is the film's second main character, Juan, who finds Little, goes on to care for him as a father figure, and offers him the love he craves. Juan, though, is a drug dealer who is supplying drugs to Little's mother. Thus, by a cruel cycle of fate, Little's savior is the same man that indirectly fuels Little's impoverished home. By Chapter 3, the adult "Black" will have essentially *become* Juan. He will make his living by dealing drugs; drive a similar classic car with the same crown on the dashboard; and wear the same black clothes, ear studs, and gold neck chain. This intergenerational cyclicity is mirrored in the film's recurring motifs of moonlight and water—specifically, in the *cycles* of the waxing and waning moon, and the corresponding ebb and flow of waves and tides.

Theme 2—The fluid, slippery nature of vulnerability and identity

Near the end of the film, Kevin, the main character's one friend, asks Black: "Who is you, man?" This questioning of identity plays a recurring role throughout the film as the main character navigates the slippery terrain of vulnerability. The division of the film into three acts reinforces this idea of fracture, or multiple potential selves. And it is water and moonlight that underscore the defining moments in which the main character is able to experience the vulnerability of being open and sensual with another person, and potentially experience the infinite nuances of love and life. In one of the film's defining scenes, where Juan teaches Little to swim in the ocean, Juan remarks that "at some point, you gotta decide for yourself who you wanna be. Can't let nobody make that decision for you." Other key moments of vulnerability and identity shaping—featuring the ocean and moonlight—include Chiron and Kevin's first kiss as well as their final tender moment at Kevin's house by the beach (a scene that ends with an ocean-and-moonlight flashback to Little as a young boy).

The slippery nature of both moonlight and water are symbolic of the fluidity and elasticity experienced *between* the otherwise rigid structures of a society in which men are supposed to interact in certain ways. This slipperiness embraces the open spectrum of feelings denied to these characters within a hypermasculine world of unyielding social rules. As he teaches Little to swim in the ocean, the gift Juan gives him is twofold: the water prepares Little for a life of waves and obstacles and teaches him to swim against them, and also opens him up to the possibilities of being vulnerable to one's own desires. Water and moonlight are thus both symbols of desire and vulnerability, and visual forms of the sonic devices through which the main characters find themselves in this coming-of-age tale.[1]

Moonlight's music: depictions of cyclicity and fluidity

The most famous example of classical music in *Moonlight* is undoubtedly Mozart's "Laudate Dominum," which we hear as Little and his school mates

---

[1] The theme of fluid identity is in part tied to the theme of cyclicity since, just like high and low tides or the waxing and waning of the moon, every character in this film embodies opposite characteristics or stereotypical character types. Thus Juan, for example, as noted earlier, is the surrogate caregiver on the one hand, but provides drugs to Little's mother on the other.

play football at the local field (0:13:20). Composed for part of a Vespers Service in the Salzburg Cathedral, "Laudate Dominum" exudes radiance, reverence, and celestial beauty. The combination of its gentle pastoral lilt—furnished largely by the gently rocking inner strings—and its simple but soaring melody is exemplary of that Godly-yet-human quality of Mozart's music so often said to define him as the universal composer situated between Bach and Beethoven. That this sacred piece of music is chosen to accompany this scene is highly significant: despite the poor neighborhood Little and the other children find themselves in (they have only a bundle of newspaper for a soccer ball), their playing together in the field constitutes their *sacred* time and space. And the musical qualities so clearly associated with Mozart as outlined above are reflected in the variety of shots used throughout the scene: the wide and high angle shots reflect the heavenly space nurtured by the music, while the shots of Little walking towards and away from the camera help establish his own point of view.

But while Mozart's music belongs to this one scene, Britell's original classical scoring continues to impact the viewer throughout the film, and it is thus on Britell's score that I will now focus. In what follows, I will track how the film's central motifs and themes are developed sonically through the score in each of the three chapters of the main character's life.

"Little's theme" (0:6:50–0:7:40)

We first hear the main musical theme—"Little's theme" for violin and piano in D major—in a diner scene where Juan, having just rescued Little, attempts to gain the boy's trust. Excepting the two penultimate bars, the harmonic content of the theme consists of a back-and-forth rocking between I and iv, foreshadowing the intergenerational cyclicity of fate that awaits the main character. Involving only semitonal movements in the inner voices, the I-iv harmonic motion also reflects the slipperiness of the moonlight and water motifs, and the fluidity of identity that will be central to this character's journey. On the one hand, the I-iv-I succession prolongs I, suggesting a state of suspension and detachment from the real world Little seeks to evade. The tonic pedal—enunciated once every two bars, like the gentle ushering of waves—heightens the feeling of nothingness, of a wash of sound smothering agency or thought. On the other hand, the alternation of major I and minor iv points to the binary components of Little's life—of a gentle and sensitive boy already destined for a life of drug dealing.

The violin likewise rocks back and forth, primarily between two notes—tonic and dominant. Its timbre—recorded close to a microphone at an extremely soft dynamic— is grainy and slippery, highlighting what will be a common sonic trait in the score: a focus on the fluidity, inbetweenness, and boundlessness of sound. That the violin doubles the piano's melodic line furthers this sense of inbetweenness since the simultaneity of percussive and sustained sounds draws our attention to the interstitial spaces of agency and sound between the attack points of the piano part.[2] And the boundlessness of sound is further enriched by the theme's beginning out of nothingness. Barely audible to begin with, it emerges from outside traffic noise.

In the theme's two penultimate bars, C# is flattened to C natural. This flattening of the leading tone softens the one point of the theme that has the potential to create intervallic tension and direction, and thus maintains the theme's contained quality. The sense of a blanket of sound is also created through attention to motif rather than clear melody. The distinctions between vamp, motif, and melody are blurred. The violin is not a clear melodic instrument, and neither is the piano; together they define the overall wash of a single melodic-harmonic soundworld.

The first two appearances of this theme occur during car rides—first toward Juan's house (0:6:50–0:7:40), and later from that house to Little's house (0:10:33–0:11:12). Set to the slipperiness of Little's musical theme, these traversals highlight the slippery cycle of Little's daily life: from drug user's house to drug dealer's house, from mother's house to surrogate mother's house, from a house of abuse to a house of nurture, and from a house of homophobia and rage to a house of acceptance.

After the first kiss (0:55:20–0:56:33)

In Chapter 2, the adolescent Chiron experiences his first kiss—alongside the ocean, and with his only friend, Kevin. Immediately afterward, we are invited to take part in Chiron's sensuous experience of feeling sand between his fingers. The slipperiness associated with this simple act is then made equally sensual in the sounds that accompany Chiron and Kevin's ride home: we hear a cyclical series of bell-like tones. These are not phrased, are often unsynchronized, and blur into each other through an echo effect—all accentuating the sensuous, rather than the formal, qualities of this series of bell tones. The bright lights we see in the dark street—resembling miniature moons—are the visual equivalents to these bells. As the light dissipates gradually from its source, and as the line between light and darkness is made indistinct, the ends of these bell tones fade into nothingness. The connection between bells and moonlight—and the cyclicity, fluidity, and boundlessness of both—is thus made explicit, reinforcing the sensuousness and vulnerability of Chiron's experience.

---

[2] I thank my student, Liam Furey, for bringing my attention to this.

Death march (1:00:25–1:02:15)

The simple joy of that loving moment is soon shattered when the school bully coerces Kevin into punching Chiron in the schoolyard. The scene opens with the bully circling both Kevin and Chiron, calling attention to the cycle of fate—a cycle that can't even be broken by true friendship.[3] Musically, "Little's Theme" is put through the "chopped and screwed" process—originally a 1990s hip hop technique, applied here to classical music—whereby the music is significantly slowed down and lowered in pitch by computer manipulations. The track is thus turned into a "death march"—here, the death is of innocence, friendship, and first love. The extremely slow tempo heightens the sense of "inbetweenness" so crucial to the aesthetic of the classical music tradition: we hear the grain and micro-variations of the instruments' timbres, and the asynchronicities of attack points are very clearly exposed. Mirroring both the economy of the film's dialog and the fractured daily moments of the film's three-act design, this technique is a sonic depiction of Chiron's vulnerability and of the exposure of his sexuality and inner world. The open sonic spaces, the magnification of the ensemble's asynchronicities, and the stimulation of our awareness of timbral change all leave blanks to be filled in, drawing our imaginations and bodily participations deep into the drama. Already slippery in nature for the reasons outlined earlier, "Little's Theme" now explores even finer shades of what lies between melodic notes and between instrumental parts; the theme is now infinitely exposed and vulnerable.

Revenge (1:03:38–1:05:20)

Chiron resolves to take control. Following an unusual high-angle shot that renders him small and vulnerable, we move to an after-shot of Chiron emerging from a sink of iced water, where he looks large, strong, and full of revenge. As he walks toward the classroom to attack the bully responsible for the bashing, we hear sporadic noises that gradually turn into the sounds of an orchestra warming up for a performance. The sonic depiction of orchestral players warming up brings with it the highly tuned sense of wonder and expectation unique to the ritual of the symphony orchestra concert. Chiron's eventual moment of revenge is thus set up as a virtuosic performance; his walk towards

---

[3] The clothing and color scheme of this scene sets up Chiron and Kevin to stand out from the other characters around them on the one hand (thus signaling their friendship), and to stand out as opposites from each other on the other hand (thus signaling the violence that the cycle of fate throws upon them). They are the only boys to be wearing polo shirts, but their color schemes are opposed: Kevin wears blue with white; Chiron wears white with blue.

the classroom resembles a concerto soloist's walk from the greenroom to the stage.

Underneath these orchestral sounds, we hear percussive, rhythmic figures articulating Chiron's determination to carry out revenge. But in a brief moment, halfway to the classroom, Chiron looks down reflectively, the percussive figures retreat, and we hear a fleeting melodic fragment of "Little's Theme"—in its original D major—emerge from the random orchestral sounds.[4] This briefest of moments recalls Chiron's childhood and the musical theme that was transformed into a death march during the schoolyard fight. Resolute in his task, though, he looks back up, the rhythmic figures return beneath the random sounds of orchestral players warming up, and Chiron enters the classroom to execute his revenge.

With Chiron's rage at boiling point, it is not surprising that music, rather than words, depicts his inner world. But once again, an exceptional type of music— here, "warm up" music existing outside of normal musical boundaries—is used to depict an exceptional state of mind.

"Black's theme" (1:10:50–1:11:32)

In Chapter 3, the adult Chiron, nicknamed "Black," is an image of his childhood father figure, Juan. We hear his theme, chopped and screwed, set to a montage of mundane activities (opening the fridge, lifting weights, doing press-ups) with his mother's voice message playing in the background—all suggestive of Black's lonely life, and of the emotional weight he still carries. Musically, Britell turns the tonic pedal—a device normally used to signal security—into a noisy disturbance, confirming Black's chaotic existence. And while the theme's melody was simple to begin with (for the most part, just two notes), it is now simplified even further, remaining static on the dominant tone. The tender ascending fourth up to the tonic note has been removed, suggesting that what was earlier a premonition of the fate of intergenerational cyclicity is now a cruel reality. Black *has* now become Juan.

Reunited (1:39:20–1:40:15)

Near the end of the film, Black and Kevin reunite, years after the incident that tore them apart. After driving back to Kevin's apartment, Chiron steps out of the car, takes in the beach, and smiles: he remembers their first kiss. Their approaching romantic moment inside Kevin's apartment will now be linked to their first kiss on the beach, with the ocean intensifying the meaning of their dialog preceding that first tender moment (Chiron: "I cry so much sometimes,

---

[4] I thank my student, Liam Furey, for bringing this moment to my attention.

I feel like I'm gonna turn into drops." Kevin: "And just roll out into the water, right?"). The love these men share for each other seems forever bound by the ocean's drum. Water functions as a symbol of Black's longing to be open to the vulnerability of Little, and to the potential of Chiron. Musically, this is reflected in the reconstitution of Black's theme. Not only is the melody fully reinstated, but a full ensemble of strings is now employed. For the first time, the theme presents as a melody rather than a series of motivic exchanges. The addition of dominant-tonic pizzicatos in the cellos aids in reshaping the function of these two notes: no longer part of an ominous cycle, they now provide forward direction to an optimistic theme.

Such thematic transformation is a hallmark of classical music. "As classical music construes its world, and ours, when melody comes back it should come back changed. Its meaning should be different … Classical melody is left to disappear, even urged to disappear, on behalf of its transformative return," asserts Kramer (2007: 38), who immediately observes: "That return is its fate; that fate is its purpose." The thematic transformations that *Moonlight*'s main classical theme undergoes, including this vital transformation near the end of the film, are essential to the viewer's emotional journey. As fine details of the score are given sensuous attention—and as suggestive worlds of interpretative space are opened up—the music gets more and more under the viewer's skin.

The final scene (1:45:39–1:46:25)

In resolution, the same bell-like sounds we heard immediately following the first kiss return. With the two men now lying together, the music forms an aural flashback to that physical connection on the beach. But that is not all. Kevin's hand under Chiron's head recalls Juan's support of Little gaining confidence in the ocean. And since bell sounds function as the sonic equivalent to moonlight and water, this provokes a visual flashback of Little as a young boy, by the ocean, in the moonlight.

Conclusion

In *Moonlight*, Britell's original score conveys the cyclicity and fluidity associated with ocean and moonlight, and it fosters the film's main themes of the cycles of life and the fluidity of identity. While popular music tracks also play an important role in the film,[5] much of the sonic articulation and

---

[5] One example is a "chopped and screwed" version of Jidenna's song "Classic Man" (1:22:09). That Black listens to this song inside his car underscores the internalization of his preoccupations with masculinity. And that we hear the song both before Black meets Kevin *and* during Black and Kevin's car ride home highlights Black's masculinity as

development of the film's motifs and themes relies on the classical score and on the techniques and associations inherent to the classical music tradition. *Moonlight's* score highlights and augments the rich, interpretative, metaphorical space characteristic of classical music, inviting viewers to fill in the sonic spaces and make the film's emotional journey their own. And this, as Kramer (2007: 42) points out, is why classical music still matters, for it "acts like a spirit in need of a body, which it finds in us when we hearken to it … These meetings leave us hungry for more … because each is by its very nature incomplete no matter how fully achieved it is in the moment."

References

Jenkins, B. 2016. *Moonlight.* A24.

Kramer, L. 2007. *Why Classical Music Still Matters.* Berkeley and Los Angeles: University of California Press.

---

important for both impressing Kevin and for rationalizing their mutual desire. Another example is the jukebox music playing in the restaurant during Black and Kevin's reunion (1:34:54). During this sensuous and intimate moment, the music plays at full volume, allowing us to enter the internal space of the characters. The 1950s jukebox-in-a-diner type song we hear, Barbara Lewis's "Hello, Stranger," signals nostalgia—in this case, the nostalgia of Black and Kevin's kiss on the beach, years ago. And the nostalgia of the more distant 1950s, where homosexual relationships were impossible, further reinforces the impossibility of Black and Kevin's love for each other.

Chapter 4

Contemporary music theater and the experience of marginalization

Federica Marsico

Ca' Foscari University of Venezia

Abstract

The paper discusses the relevance of contemporary music theater in the frame of classical music's role in society, claiming that entering into contact with music can enrich people's existences and broaden our horizons of experience. The paper focuses on Sylvano Bussotti, who stood out for his provocative breaking of sexual taboos and for his explicit representation of homoeroticism and diverse gender identities. Through a review of some of Bussotti's works, the paper highlights the subversive power of music theater, arguing that classical music can relate experiences of marginalization and challenge discriminatory prejudices.

Keywords: Sylvano Bussotti, music and homosexuality, queer musicology, 20th-century music theater

* * *

The vitality of classical music manifests itself without filters to the musicologist who deals with the output of artists of the second half of the twentieth century who have chosen this genre to place themselves critically in the society. Through classical music, these authors tell the contemporary world, which pulsates like a living organism in the notes of their compositions and runs like lifeblood in their scores. However, their works often do not appear in concert programs because of their provocative charge and fall by the wayside.

A composition that has never been played after its debut and that survives only as a musical score can be brought back to life by the investigative and hermeneutic action of a musicologist. This kind of research can constitute a first step toward renewing the interest of audiences, interpreters, and institutions involved in supporting and disseminating musical culture. Musicologists play a key role in the re-evaluation of an artwork, making the target audience aware of its worth and, in some cases, of the conditions that hindered its aesthetic reception. This mediation is far from simple, but, if successful, can significantly contribute to proving that classical music is still alive and vibrant. Such a task becomes more challenging in our contemporary world, where music is increasingly turned into a consumer good that saturates our senses, whether it is blasting in a shopping center or through a small but powerful loudspeaker while we are chilling in the park.

The task of the musicologist who seeks to bring classical music out of the realm of experts and specialists in order to ensure its vitality within our society becomes all the more urgent when the composer is someone who aims to enter a dialog with our contemporary time. And when the themes at the heart of this dialog are taboo in the author's culture, the artwork breaks through in all its topical vitality. The composer's dialectical relationship with his or her cultural context, however, as it emerges from the themes addressed, may relegate him or her to a marginal position with respect to the artists celebrated within the dominant culture. In this case, the composer's works may fail to be acknowledged and disseminated, and fail to find their place in the cultural mainstream.

The work of Sylvano Bussotti (b. Florence, 1931) vividly illustrates how the themes of an artist's production can determine his or her position in the art world. The last living Italian witness of the great European fervor that followed the arrival of John Cage (who was a good friend of his), Bussotti can boast an artistic career that ran through the twentieth century and the early 2000s. He worked with interpreters of the caliber of Cathy Berberian and David Tudor and brushed shoulders with the most sophisticated international musicians, directors, painters, writers, and intellectuals of his time.[1] Moreover, Bussotti is one of those rare truly multifaceted artists, working since the beginning of his career not only as a composer, but also as a writer, librettist, director, stage and costume designer, and even as an actor in his own plays (Bussotti, 1982, 1986, 1997, 2002, 2016). In the 1970s, he enjoyed considerable success in France, where he was the subject of a retrospective during *Semaines musicales internationales de Paris* in 1970, organized by Maurice Fleuret, and of a monographic session during the eleventh edition of the *Festival international d'art contemporain de Royan* in 1974, organized by Harry Halbreich and Paul Beusen. In Italy, some of his major institutional recognitions include his

---

[1] For an introduction to this artist, see Bucci, 1988; Esposito, 2013; Osmond-Smith, 2001; Scarlini, 2010.

nomination as artistic director of Teatro La Fenice in the 1970s and of the Venice Biennale between the 1980s and 1990s.

Despite his brilliant career, Bussotti today does not enjoy the recognition he deserves among musicologists, unlike slightly older Italian composers such as Bruno Maderna, Luciano Berio, and Luigi Nono. If, on the one hand, this relative neglect is due to the tendency to historicize authors only after their death, on the other hand Bussotti's open challenge to sexual taboos in music theater, a genre in which he was extremely active, seemed almost to inhibit critical attention.[2] When approaching Bussotti's production, one cannot overlook the fact that his open homosexuality, which he displayed without the slightest inhibition (Attinello et al., 2007), significantly contributed to an aesthetic in which the private sphere intervenes in the artwork and shapes it, disrupting any separation between the author's art and his biography. A case in point is the melodrama *Lorenzaccio* (Venice, Teatro La Fenice, 1972), where the incipit of Vincenzo Monti's famous Italian translation of the *Iliad* is changed in order to make explicit the composer's relationship with his then partner Romano Amidei, to whom the opera is dedicated. The original verses are transformed from "Cantami, o Diva, del Pelide Achille | l'ira funesta che infiniti addusse | lutti agli Achei" ("Sing to me, oh goddess, of the fatal wrath of Achilles, Peleus's son, which brought countless woes upon the Achaeans") into "Cantami o Musa-Diva-Musica | del Divino Amore-Eroe | la carne aperta | viva Romano" ("Sing to me, oh Muse, goddess of Music, of the open flesh of the divine Love-Hero, long live Romano") (Bussotti, 1972, III: 3).

This is just one of many cases where homoeroticism is connected to autobiographical elements in Bussotti's productions, often by means of a play with polysemy (Marsico, 2020b). For instance, in the seventh movement of the opera-ballet *Nuit du faune*,[3] composed between 1990 and 1991, the orchestral introduction is followed by a short monolog that begins with a quote from Stéphane Mallarmé's *Monologue d'un faune* (1865).[4] The verse "L'illusion, Sylvain, a-t-elle les yeux bleus et verts" ("Does illusion, Sylvan, have blue or green eyes") becomes, in the Italian version, "Silvano l'illusione ha gli occhi blu | ha l'illusione gli occhi azzurri | e verdi" ("Silvano, does illusion have blue eyes, blue and green eyes"), making the autobiographical element explicit: "Silvano"

---

[2] After the first pioneering studies (La Face, 1974; Maehder, 1984), the literature dedicated to Bussotti's production includes: Attinello, 1992, 2005; Evangelista, 2013; Iotti, 2014; Maehder, 1991, 2003; Marsico, 2017, 2019a, 2019b, 2020a, forthcoming a, forthcoming b; Morelli, 2009; Tortora, 2013, 2020; Ulman, 1996.

[3] Bussotti, 1991: 15-19 (pages 16-17 are missing—page 18 is on the back of page 15—so the passage is three pages long).

[4] For the complete text see Mallarmé, 1983: 180–190.

is the name of the god of the woods, but it is also the name of the composer. Later in the monolog, the verse "si ce faune rencontre Querelle …" makes reference to the protagonist of Jean Genet's novel *Querelle de Brest*, famous for its explicit description of gay love, and thereby reveals the author's homoerotic desire.

The most provocative aspect of Bussotti's music theater lies in the exhibition of the interpreters' sinuous and half-naked bodies, enhanced by brightly colored costumes. It is no coincidence that, in the mid-1970s, Bussotti developed a long-term theatrical project titled "Bussotti Opera Ballet" which merged traditional opera with ballet to create a performance in which dance and autobiography are as essential to the dramaturgy as is music. The central figure of these performances was often Rocco (Rocco Quaglia off-stage), a dancer and Bussotti's companion. Rocco was the one who inspired the lavish costume designed for the role of Osiris in *Oggetto amato*, and who interpreted Mino, Michelangelo's faithful apprentice during his work on the Sistine chapel, in *Nottetempo*, performed as a diptych with the previous work at the Teatro Lirico in Milan in 1976 for the official inauguration of the Bussotti Opera Ballet. Rocco also played the role of the gigolo Hippolyte, who seduces the clients of a gay brothel, in *Le Racine: pianobar pour Phèdre* (Marsico, 2020a); he starred in many other roles until his retirement. To Bussotti, Rocco epitomized the height of seduction and the object of his desire, removed from the private dimension and shared with the public.

Some people among the audience, however, were hardly inclined to acknowledge the existence of this kind of desire in the real world, let alone give it the same dignity as straight love. By celebrating the male body on stage, Bussotti was conveying the message that gay love coexists with straight love, that it is neither a sin nor a perversion, and that gay people have the right to live, enjoy themselves, and be happy just like anybody else. He addressed a country where homophobia remained deeply rooted, despite the absence of an explicitly discriminatory legislation. (Just remember the unfair judicial persecution of the gay writer Aldo Braibanti in 1968 (Bompiani et al., 1969) and the cruel murder of a young gay couple in Sicily in 1980 (Rossi Barilli, 1999)). The cultural influence of the Catholic Church has undeniably contributed (although it is not the only cause) to make it difficult to promote the social equality of homosexuals in Italy, which to this day is home to associations that follow scientifically unfounded theories about curing homosexuality. Bussotti's music theater therefore carries a strong political and cultural message.

Bussotti's provocation against Italy's self-righteous mentality and indifference to issues of sexual discrimination was carried out through one of the farthest-reaching genres of classical music, namely musical theater. The latter's intrinsic multimedia nature—based on the marriage of music, poetry, and *mise en scène*—gives the artist a communication tool that no other genre can provide. Bussotti was therefore able to prod the sensitive nerves of a nation still entrenched in prejudice and discrimination. That is why his theater disturbed and irritated a large portion of the audience, disgusted at the sight of the shamelessly exhibited male body. See, for instance, this scolding review of the premiere of *Le Racine*, published in a major Italian daily newspaper:

> Three long acts, lavishly or even palpably boring, overloaded with cold eroticism and crammed with exposed buttocks that are given the prominence usually assigned to the protagonists: three acts of calligraphic elegance, celebrating a bad taste that transforms into trash even the velvets and silks of the costumes [...]. There are also a few scenic elements of convoluted and gratuitous obscenity which can be explained only by tastes that have nothing to do with art.[5]

To Bussotti, bringing the audience to witness the breaking of one of our society's more deeply rooted taboos, namely eroticism in general and homoeroticism in particular, was an important social and political mission, which, however, was likely to meet with disapproval from a part of the public.[6] He took up the challenge, however. And today, it is up to us to understand the value of his work as a composer. Musicologists, who have the necessary interpretive tools to uncover the role of the musical theater in contemporary society, are called upon to break prejudices and to assess Bussotti's work as art.

To end on an autobiographical note. Over the years that I spent studying the figure of Bussotti, who is mentioned in the literature on the avant-garde music of the second half of the twentieth century almost exclusively for his pictographic scores, I have thoroughly investigated his catalog and discovered several titles that open up reflection on the relationship between music and highly topical issues such as non-normative gender identity, homosexuality, and homophobia. Many of his compositions have no longer—or very rarely— been performed after their debut. As a consequence, the scholar of Bussotti ends up working on someone considered to be a marginal composer within the canon of avant-garde music. As I wondered about the reasons why an

---

[5] "Tre lunghi atti, di una noia sontuosa e addirittura palpabile, sovraccarichi di erotismo freddo, fitti di natiche esposte col rilievo che spetta agli elementi protagonisti: tre atti di calligrafica eleganza all'insegna d'un cattivo gusto che trasforma in ciarpame perfino i velluti e le sete dei costumi [...]. Vi sono anche eventi scenici di lambiccata, e gratuita, sconcezza, a chiarire i quali occorre chiamare in soccorso altre predilezioni, che non quella per l'arte" (Celli, 1980). The full article is included in Marsico, 2020a: 188.

[6] For example, the cries of protest on the occasion of the first performance of *Nottetempo* are explanatory of this disapproval, see Bussotti 2020.

otherwise successful artist should be received this way, it gradually became clear to me that Bussotti does not have a prominent position in the canon of the second half of the twentieth century because the themes that he brought onto the stage were themselves marginalized by society. The flipside of this reception process, however, is that Bussotti's classical music is more alive than ever because it talks about our own lives, and about the life of the author, and is impregnated with the reality that surrounds us. Although some of his works have not enjoyed the favor of artistic producers, they have never lost their vitality. Bringing them back on stage today, therefore, does not amount to bringing them back to life, but to granting them the unprejudiced recognition that they deserve.

References

Attinello, P. 1992. "Signifying Chaos: A Semiotic Analysis of Sylvano Bussotti's *Siciliano.*" *Repercussions* 1(2): 84–110.

--------2005. "Hieroglyph, Gesture, Sign, Meaning: Bussotti's *Pièces de Chair II.*" In Roger A. Kendall and Roger W. H. Savage (eds.). *Perspectives in Systematic Musicology.* Los Angeles: University of California Press: 219–227.

Attinello, P. and D. Osmond-Smith. 2007. "Gay Darmstadt: Flamboyance and Rigor at the Summer Courses for New Music." *Contemporary Music Review* 26(1): 105–114.

Bompiani, G., E. Umberto, A. Gatti, M. Gozzano, A. Moravia, and C. Musatti. 1969. *Sotto il nome di plagio: studi e interventi sul caso Braibanti.* Milano: Bompiani.

Bucci, M. (ed.). 1988. *L'opera di Sylvano Bussotti: musica, segno, immagine, progetto, il teatro, le scene, i costumi, gli attrezzi ed i capricci dagli anni Quaranta al Bussotti Opera Ballet.* Firenze: Electa.

Bussotti, S. 1972. *Lorenzaccio: melodramma romantico danzato in 5 atti, 23 scene e 2 fuoriprogramma in omaggio al dramma omonimo di Alfred de Musset.* Milano: Ricordi.

--------1982. *I miei teatri: diario segreto, diario pubblico, alcuni saggi.* Palermo: Novecento.

--------1986. *Letterati ignoranti: poesie per musica: con un disegno dell'autore.* Siena: Quaderni di Barbablù.

--------1991. *Nuit du faune: concerti con figure* (prima versione per Francoforte). Milano: Ricordi.

--------1997. *Non fare il minimo rumore: 29 poesie e una prosa 1982–1997 (con due disegni dell'autore).* Ravenna: Edizioni del Girasole.

--------2002. *Disordine alfabetico: musica, pittura, teatri, scritture (1957–2002).* Milano: Spirali.

--------2016. *Prose, sonetti e poesie.* Torino: Coup d'idée Edizioni d'Arte.

--------2020. BOB Bussotti Opera Ballet. YouTube: https://www.youtube.com/watch?v=4mnry8XWSVM. Accessed November 30, 2020.

Celli, T. 1980. "Fedra in fricassea: *Le Racine* di Bussotti alla Piccola Scala." *Il Messaggero*, December 11, p. 12.

Esposito, L. 2013. *Un male incontenibile: Sylvano Bussotti, artista senza confini.* Milano: Bietti.

Evangelista, M. 2013. "Teatri nascosti: gesto, segno e drammaturgia nell'opera di Sylvano Bussotti." *Civiltà Musicale* 23: 67–68.

Iotti, D. 2014. *L'"aura" ritrovata: il teatro di Sylvano Bussotti da* La Passion selon Sade *a* Lorenzaccio. Lucca: Libreria Musicale Italiana.

La Face, G. 1974. "Teatro, eros e segno nell'opera di Sylvano Bussotti." *Rivista Italiana di Musicologia* 9: 250–268.

Maehder, J. 1984. "Sviluppi della drammaturgia musicale bussottiana." *Nuova Rivista Musicale Italiana* 18(3): 441–468.

--------1991. "'Odo un Sylvano': Zur Rolle des Komponisten, Regisseurs, Bühnen—und Kostümbildners Sylvano Bussotti im zeitgenössischen Musiktheater," Frankfurt am Main, Alte Oper (program book for *Nuit du faune*): 16–63.

--------2003. "Zitat, Collage, Palimpsest: Zur Textbasis des Musiktheaters bei Luciano Berio und Sylvano Bussotti." In H. Danuser and M. Kassel (eds.). *Musiktheater heute: Internationales Symposion der Paul Sacher Stiftung: Basel 2001.* Mainz: Schott: 97–133.

Mallarmé, S. 1983. *Œuvres complétes*, ed. by C. P. Barbier and C.G. Millan. Paris: Flammarion, Vol. 1.

Marsico, F. 2017. "A Queer Approach to the Classical Myth of Phaedra in Music." *Kwartalnik Młodych Muzykologów UJ* 34(3): 7–28.

--------2019a. "Da *Le Racine* a *Fedra* di Sylvano Bussotti: riscrittura di un libretto metateatrale." In I. Bonomi, E. Buroni and E. Sala (eds.). *La librettologia, crocevia interdisciplinare: problemi e prospettive.* Milano: Ledizioni: 129–144.

--------2019b. "Il libretto di *Le Racine: pianobar pour Phèdre* (1980) di Sylvano Bussotti: le fonti e la drammaturgia." *Acta Musicologica* 91(1): 71–96.

--------2020a. *La seduzione queer di Fedra: il mito secondo Britten, Bussotti e Henze.* Roma: Aracne.

--------2020b. "Le provocazioni di *Le Racine*: l'erotismo 'selon' Sylvano Bussotti." In D. Tortora (ed.), *The Theatres of Sylvano Bussotti.* Turnhout: Brepols: 277–298.

--------Forthcoming a. "La prospettiva di Sylvano Bussotti nella ricezione novecentesca di Monteverdi." In G. Borio and A. Carone (eds.). *Echi monteverdiani nel Novecento italiano.* Venezia: Fondazione Cini.

--------Forthcoming b. "Un'opera dimenticata di un *contestataire contesté*: *Syro Sadun Settimino* di Sylvano Bussotti." *Studi Musicali* 12(1) n.s.

Morelli, G. 2009. *Dopo il melodramma: il teatro lirico di Sylvano Bussotti.* Pisa: ETS.

Osmond-Smith, D. 2001. "Sylvano Bussotti." In S. Sadie and J. Tyrrell (eds.). *The New Grove Dictionary of Music and Musicians.* London: Macmillan, Vol. 4: 678–682.

Rossi Barilli, G. 1999. *Il movimento gay in Italia.* Milano: Feltrinelli.

Scarlini, L. 2010. *Corpi da musica: vita e teatro di Sylvano Bussotti.* Firenze: Maschietto.

Tortora, D. 2013. "Da *selon Sade* a *La Passion selon X*: intorno alla *Passion selon Sade* di Sylvano Bussotti." *Studi Musicali* 4(1): 203–235.

--------2020. *The Theatres of Sylvano Bussotti.* Turnhout: Brepols.

Ulman, E. 1996. "The Music of Sylvano Bussotti." *Perspectives of New Music* 34(2): 186–201.

Chapter 5

Relevance and meaning: classical music in the present

Natalie Tsaldarakis

City, University of London

Abstract

The paper begins with two remarks: first, 2020 is Beethoven's 250th anniversary, despite most of the scheduled events being cancelled; and secondly, the musicologist Leech-Wilkinson has asserted through social media that "classical music performance has nothing to say about current concerns" ("current concerns" remaining in need of a more precise contextualization, of course). The paper tackles claims that classical music is insular and irrelevant by also considering Lawrence Kramer's writings and reframes musical works as a mirror (of/for its audiences) whose meaning is renewed with every listening.

Keywords: Lawrence Kramer, Daniel Leech-Wilkinson, classical music and relevance, Beethoven's *Ruins of Athens*, Leonidas Kavakos

* * *

This paper is a response to the central question of the continued vitality of classical music. It is underpinned by two closely linked events: firstly, the celebration this year of Beethoven's 250th birthday, and, secondly, the assertion by the musicologist Daniel Leech-Wilkinson that "classical performance has nothing to say about current concerns" (Leech-Wilkinson 2020a). Ultimately, this paper is both a critical response to Leech-Wilkinson's implication that the current culture of classical music itself, in part, but not wholly, due to its dominant mode of performance, is insular and irrelevant as well as a commentary on the state and place of classical music in the modern world.

Leech-Wilkinson caused quite a furor with his recent communications via social media. In turn he received criticism in no uncertain terms from professional musicians and the general public alike. Peter Donohoe tweeted that Leech-Wilkinson's claim is "twaddle"; the violinist Miles Golding, a trustee of the Harpenden Music Foundation, retorted that his spirits had "just now" been lifted by "dead white male" Beethoven courtesy of the "effervescent," "exhilarating," and "extraordinary" finale of the String Quartet Op. 18, no. 3— "Effing genius"; and the composer Des Oliver responded that the claim of irrelevance to "current concerns" (in particular to the COVID-19 pandemic, to which Leech-Wilkinson was referring) is "bizarre," and tartly asked what Shakespeare or Rembrandt had to say about the coronavirus (Oliver 2020). In the discussion below, it will become apparent that classical music, its performance, the composition as a musical work, and the score as the compositional conception's written evidence are different, yet often overlapping, concepts that add to the confusion while also bringing to the fore some key preconceptions and attitudes within the music's milieu.

Leech-Wilkinson (2009, 2020), but also in various degrees Nicholas Cook (2014) and other critics of the historically informed performance movement (commonly referred to as HIP), find that the classical performing world nowadays generally seeks to ascertain the authority of the composer, and view the score as the gateway to a single, viable, and authentic performance of the work. Both Leech-Wilkinson and Cook have also written on the matter as part of their previous work for the Centre for the History and Analysis of Recorded Music (CHARM, 2009), and both claim this view of the musical work and its realization in performance is widely shared and highly policed. Cook (2014: 400), for example, writes:

> Performance practices fall through the gaps between words; they are like the soft tissues that disappear when animals are fossilized. Consequently glib assumptions that we have any secure understanding of how music sounded in past centuries cannot be sustained. [...] All this creates a strong suspicion that what is really being policed is current performance practice, propped up by claims of historical authenticity that are selective at best and self-seeking at worst. But the real question is not how well supported these claims are. It is why in music, and apparently only in music, we should make so strong—though selective—an assumption that, if something went one way then, it must go the same way now.[1]

---

[1] See also Dorottya Fabian's discussion of music performance literature that presents the main ideas on HIP and modernism as expressed by Taruskin, Leech-Wilkinson, and others (*A Musicology of Performance: Theory and Method Based on Bach's Solos for Violin,* 2014: 25-74).

Leech-Wilkinson's claim about performance, like Cook's, is a reflection of the perennial struggle between historical consciousness and contemporary relevance. His critique is premised upon the view that the original meaning of historical music is no longer available to us, divorced from the society in which it came into being, especially in the absence of recordings from that time, and instead derives from the ways in which its musical content has been reproduced over time: "What [scores] mean depends on how they sound to people, and how they sound to people depends on the configuration of their minds; and that is not just a historical issue. […]. How it sounds before our own time is something we cannot know in nearly enough detail without recordings." In a way, Leech-Wilkinson finds this auditory lack to be both a limitation and a liberating aspect of music as it reconfigures itself in the mind to continue to move people (CHARM, 2009). The main thrust of Leech-Wilkinson and Cook's positions is that classical music's meaning should be liberated from the constraints of a search for authenticity, which is variously criticized as the source of policing and alienation from modern audiences (Leech-Wilkinson, 2020). Similarly, they seek to reverse a perceived hierarchy which privileges the composer over the performer (Cook, 2014: 402), the further identified problem being the lack of "the pluralism that was so prominent a feature of nineteenth-century musical culture" (Cook, 2014: 401).

For Leech-Wilkinson (2020), any and all performances should be explored for their viability. In the introduction to his latest online publication, we read that his research "on performance style and how it changes, led him step by step to the belief that there must be yet more—perhaps far more—ways of performing scores persuasively than have been explored to date." Even more importantly, Leech-Wilkinson asserts that "there are no valid criteria for evaluating performances other than the extent to which they move or excite or interest or fascinate us as we listen" (2020). The potential reception of these different musical performances is the substance of further interesting discussion which falls outside the scope of the present paper and was also the object of Leech-Wilkinson's earlier experiments, which Cook (2014) says were conducted by employing "what might be seen as perverse performance practices, such as playing repertory pieces two or three times faster or slower than would normally be considered acceptable—which inevitably has knock-on effects for other parameters" (Cook, 2014: 400). For Leech-Wilkinson, musical scores have limited value in reproducing faithful performances in sound: "The habits the composer assumed are not encoded in the score. They are lost. The notes in the score are all there is. And they are just notes." But the scores remain rich in potential as a starting point for creativity (Leech-Wilkinson, 2020). By contrast, other musicologists, such as Lawrence Kramer, believe (without denying the incompleteness of the score) that music itself is a source of historical knowledge and should be treated as a primary source (2005).

The boldly stated position as seen in Leech-Wilkinson's social media post inadvertently proclaims classical music's irrelevance to modern society, and was certainly understood in this context by Peter Donohoe, the concert pianist at the receiving end, and by many of those who sought to respond. The charge *seems* to be directed only at the rigidity of performance requirements, but it actually goes much further. In Leech-Wilkinson's *What's Wrong with Classical Music*, classical music is addressed beyond the repertoire via a far more complex and all-encompassing view of its world, including its actors in their broadest sense, its audience, the score, and its performance. Echoing a similar position taken by Richard Taruskin (Cook, 2014: 399), Leech-Wilkinson regards the composition as a simple set of instructions and claims that after the composer's death there is "no ethical obligation at all to continue to perform in the original manner" (Leech-Wilkinson, 2020). A paragraph addressing how "classical music constructs Utopias" makes it evident that the criticism is not only narrowly directed at the performance practices per se, but also at everyone and everything that contributes to the perpetuation of a stagnant status quo.[2] Furthermore, if Leech-Wilkinson's position constitutes a sweeping charge against the modern classical music world and the performances it sanctions, this is certainly in keeping with his previous research criticizing the HIP movement (2009), which he considers the very cause for the increasing irrelevance of classical music to modern audiences. In fact, he proposes that by abandoning HIP's narrow view of the score and resultant policing of performance, and by espousing innovation instead, the score "may mean something new: and it seems very likely that new audiences will be attracted to classical music, reversing its decline" (2020). In my view, Leech-Wilkinson seeks to affirm the music against those who he sees as its abusers, and yet in the process, there seems to be an implied, but unacknowledged, attack on the music itself emanating from his argument. I shall return to the matter of policing and meaning later.

Leech-Wilkinson's position receives a more detailed response in my Ph.D. thesis because his claims are central to questions about pianistic traditions

---

[2] See, for example, the paragraph on cultural power which ends with the sentence "There is rivalry, of course, enough to keep teachers' pupils loyal, enough to see other teachers' classes as Other, but not enough for critics or similarly ideologically invested audiences to see any one of these micro-schools of playing as deviant." The accompanying diagram is captioned *The pressures on performers to conform*, and maps the "Normative Concert Life" which connects critics, agents, promoters, and others, to competitions, to what he calls "micro-schools of performance."

which are fundamental to my research.[3] However, instead of reiterating my critique here, I will focus on further aspects of meaning, communication, performance, conformity, and relevance.

The musical work as a communication, the competent audience, and its expectations as context

It is my position that for a musical or other work of art of the past to be successful, it has to have the ability to resonate on its own terms with modern audiences. Its communication requires an artist-composer who is both skilled and inspired, a performer of similar description, and importantly, an audience which ideally is versed in the idiom presented by the composer through the performer, or is at least receptive to engaging with it.[4]

The limited scope of the present paper prevents me from delving into the highly nuanced commentary provided by Fabian on the differences in performance between the modernists (HIP) and the postmodernists, and between the classical-modernists and romantic-modernists (2015: 3–35). However, for me, contrary to Leech-Wilkinson, the problem is ultimately not one of an enforced conformity that prevents repeated performances from sparking excitement in declining audiences. It is the problem of ensuring that we continue to cultivate basic familiarity and understanding in the audience. I think this is perhaps the most important factor in keeping classical music current. In the case of historical repertoire, alienation would occur only if there were no listeners left willing to at least engage with the music's surface, or worse, no competent performers left to present it. Of course, what constitutes a competent performer may also be debatable in light of the disagreements between the HIP practitioners and its critics. However, the issue in this case is still not so much one of relevance as it is of education, funding, and dissemination. Furthermore, as we find ourselves in the midst of the pandemic with concert halls closed until 2022 in some countries, these issues are forcefully being brought to the fore as dissemination, training, and performance environments are forced to renegotiate their very viability online or in altered, physically distanced modes of presentation. We are at a momentous time in our history which directly affects the modes of

---

[3] On authenticity, see Ian Pace's (2013) on the hierarchy among the composer, the work, and its interpreter, as well as his "The New State of Play" in *Performance Studies* (2017: 281-292).

[4] See also Peter Kivy's discussion of the premises for a successful performance in his *Authenticities* (1995).

communication at the core of music performance, and which, I expect, will cause major shifts in both performance and scholarship.

Besides the ever-changing, physical or virtual, social-cultural environment in which music sounds, the context of a musical work also needs to be considered, and this may be understood as part of what is expected of a competent listener. Such is the case, for example in Schubert's avoidance of the tonic key during much of his Lied "Erlkönig," as discussed in Kramer's exchange with Rose Rosengard Subotnik (1979). This avoidance may be interpreted in a way that departs from Subotnik's view of it as simply weakening the tonal structure. In light of its audience's assumption and strong expectation of the tonic, Schubert's avoidance of it may be calculated to cause anxiety in order to parallel the anxiety the father and the son in the text both feel about the ever-present Erlkönig. Therefore, in this instance, meaning has not become less clear because a norm has been disregarded. Rather, Schubert was writing for an audience brought up musically in the same classical diatonic tradition he himself knew. His innovation in loosening the tonic does not result in alienating his audiences or dissociating meaning, but rather in creating the effect of psychological disturbance. In other words, Schubert, like the Romantics who followed him, still worked from a premise of strong tonal expectations clearly understood by their competent audiences. These composers understood what was expected or customary and, by delaying the fulfillment of such expectations or by completely eschewing them, reveled in the resulting harmonic surprise and emotional power.

The historical distance between modern audiences and older repertoire from past eras before the advent of recording makes this an especially important point to make: Leech-Wilkinson welcomes disregard for norms in the quest for new meaning, and invites the performer to partake in this process.[5] However, the testing of compositional norms is part of the composer's role, rather than that of the performer. This has become apparent as there has been a gradual shift from composers who performed their own works (most notably pianists and violinists such as Paganini, Liszt, Brahms, Rachmaninoff, and others) to modern interpreters who do not compose and, conversely, composers who do not perform. The tonal procedure has to be considered separately from the issue of performance practice if the integrity of the original composition is to be maintained. Therefore, any performance, as an act of interpretation, needs to incorporate the process of understanding and transmitting the tonal procedure to the competent listeners. The only manner in which Leech-

---

[5] For example, see Leech-Wilkinson's description of the workshop on Dido & *Belinda* (2020).

Wilkinson's approach to performance can be legitimized is by assigning it its proper label, namely, that of arrangements, in the glorious but separate tradition that counts Ferruccio Busoni, Franz Liszt, Leopold Godowsky, and many others among its contributors.

Structure, autonomy, and the power of emotion

The foregoing approach to tonality and composition reframes Subotnik's view that meaning in music is derived directly from the autonomous musical structure. I do not dispute the autonomy of the work in the limited sense of its existence on paper or sound, separate from the composer when completed, and separate from performers and audiences, ready to be rediscovered when fallen in obscurity. But meaning stems from the listeners' minds according to their degree of knowledge of the musical idiom on hand. It is perhaps this matter, which is not addressed by Leech-Wilkinson, that makes me skeptical about his criticisms. A private communication with Kramer (via email, July 5, 2020), led to the following interesting clarification, which is important to bear in mind considering that his exchange with Subotnik dates from 1979: "[This] very early article…equates musical autonomy and musical intelligibility and argues against an argument by Rose Subotnik that nineteenth-century art music suffered a joint loss of both. My later work entirely repudiates the equation and rejects the concept of autonomy." In short, and from the perspective of Kramer's work since 1990, listener competence and the ability to derive meaning is a matter of intelligibility rather than autonomy, which as he states is nonexistent.

However, the further problem I found with Subotnik's response to Kramer is that she did not acknowledge the power of emotion in oratorical gestures.[6] She underestimates the emotional power of the musical gesture within a well-conceived structure to arouse emotive responses in audiences and to allow for engagement even by less well-versed listeners, thus also ensuring classical music's ability to maintain its relevance. The problem is especially evident in her discussion of Beethoven's Fifth Symphony and its use of repetition in the return of Scherzo material on the oboe in the last movement (mm.172 ff.), which she narrowly labels as expressing doubt (1979: 156–157). Many other writers have interpreted this famous passage with greater richness of meaning, including Kramer himself (1984: 237–240), who subsequently wrote of the passage as a return to a "liminal defile" of indefinite space and time, rendered uncanny by the omission of the earlier basses and timpani, and harking further back to the oboe cadenza of the first movement. But examples can be

---

[6] For an in-depth discussion specifically of Beethoven as orator, see Barth (1992: 420).

multiplied. Barry Cooper (2000: 184) found the recollection to be a confirmation of "the sense of progress from darkness to light, tragedy to joy, struggle to victory." Donald Francis Tovey (quoted in Muxfeldt, 2011: 128) saw it as the return of a painful memory from the past on the march to triumph:

> Let us remember that the "scherzo" had a tremendous emotional value, and then consider how it is to be reintroduced into the sustained triumph of the finale. [..] We can easily see, now that Beethoven has shown us, that his is the one true solution which confirms the truth of the former terror and the security of the present triumph; but no lesser an artist could have found it. Beethoven recalls the third movement as a memory which we know for a fact, but can no longer understand: there is now a note of self-pity, for which we had no leisure when the terror was upon our souls: the depth and darkness are alike absent, and in the dry light of day we cannot remember our fears of the unknown.

Drawing upon Tovey's comments, Kristina Muxfeldt (2011: 129) similarly viewed this passage as a recollection of past distress as triumph draws closer:

> Beethoven's return emulates a familiar perceptual process, the intrusion of an unforgettably suspenseful past event into the experience of a more secure, predictable present. [...] The final measures of Beethoven's highly pressurized buildup into the recapitulation are indeed a close, and only slightly abbreviated, facsimile of the earlier event, as if, in drawing closer again to the present triumph, the recollection had finally gained access to some of the original emotion.

And behind all of these descriptions hovers a famous passage from E. M. Forster's novel *Howard's End* (1910), which treats the recollection as a march of nihilistic "goblins" that, however dispelled, could always return *again*:

> The goblins were scattered. He brought back the gusts of splend[or], the heroism, the youth, the magnificence of life and of death, and, amid vast roarings of a superhuman joy, he led his Fifth Symphony to its conclusion. But the goblins were there. They could return. He had said so bravely, and that is why one can trust Beethoven when he says other things.

Meaning reassigned, or displaced

With the passing of time, meaning changes or is often assigned anew. An extreme example of this would be the result of historical amnesia or pure ignorance: there will always be people who find music, irrespective of provenance, amusing or calming. For example, Baroque dances designed for palace life can provoke the criticism that they are remnants of a degenerate, oppressive, imperialist culture. However, to the people who find the sounds and rhythms of these dances amusing or entertaining and who are unaware of the music's specific socio-historical context or compositional processes, the claim of irrelevance itself becomes irrelevant. Such repurposing of music stands at the center of the marketing efforts of media outlets that try to make classical music cool or approachable or profitable. An example is the well-known British radio station Classic FM, which states on its website: "We believe classical music can and should be a part of everyone's lives [...] To achieve this, the station plays familiar music alongside less-known pieces, all chosen to uplift, soothe, and stir the emotions" (About Classic FM, 2020).

Certainly Classic FM's digital album *50 Bathtime Classics* cannot claim to reflect its composers' original intentions: Barber's Adagio for Strings Op. 11/2, Faure's "In Paradisum," the second movement of Mendelssohn's Violin Concerto, and the aria from J. S. Bach's Goldberg Variations BWV 988 are all part of this album. Nor is this an isolated example as there is a long list of such digital albums, most with utilitarian titles. *For Babies, Chill-Out, Smooth Classics, Mother's Day, For Children, Relaxing Classics*, and *Dinner Party Classics* are just some of the offerings. These collections change, or at least shape, the perceived meaning and purpose of art music by treating it as a commodity in terms that go well beyond the immediate sales of tickets, recordings, or scores. They represent a perhaps unpalatable, yet still pertinent, example of renewed relevance and meaning stemming from sources other than the original intentions and milieus of the music's composers. Moreover, in some cases meaning is achieved only later on. I am reminded, for example, of the dissonant work of Ives: dissonant not only compositionally, but also to the society to which he belonged, and obviously dissonant to the expectations of its audiences. Compositions such as his Piano Sonata no. 2, "Concord Mass., 1840–1860," which was composed 1911–1915, published 1920, premiered 1938, and was first released over 30 years later on Columbia records in 1948, found meaning and acceptance only belatedly.

Conformity, criticism, the importance of culture, personal meaning, and the work as mirror

The idea of gatekeepers and imposed conformity to a single idealized performance, which as mentioned in the opening paragraphs of this paper is central to Leech-Wilkinson's critique, also arises within the milieu of competitions (Leech-Wilkinson, 2020). However, competitions do not determine the reality of professional performance, despite their valuable function as launch pads for the careers of artists. Competitions seek to ascertain an elite level of performance by quantifying the performers' skills. As such, they have a specific, important, yet narrowly circumscribed, function. Leech-Wilkinson asserts the rigidity of the wider classical performance culture beyond the competition circuit based on an observation by Bruce Haynes (2007: 6): "Any good young instrumentalist knows how each piece is expected to be played, right down to bowings, dynamic marks, and places to breathe."

However, this claim of the premium placed on conformity is contradicted by Leech-Wilkinson's own assertion that the performance style of the well-known violinist Patricia Kopatchinskaja successfully breaks with convention: "This is playing in which extremes beyond the conventional range play a vital expressive role, allowing her to reveal the expressive potential in scores that we may be dimly aware of, but that no one else, until now, has been able to turn so vividly into sound" (2020). If classical music and its performers are being policed, as the musicologist contends, how has this violinist come to rank among the recognized virtuosos of her generation? Although admittedly the researcher asserts that such examples exist in small numbers, he does not explain how the enforced conformity he sees and criticizes allows for the few original artists to rise to the top of their profession regardless.

Leech-Wilkinson's idea that classical music under its current regime of performance is declining, dead, or irrelevant is particularly puzzling and worrisome for its potential to become a self-fulfilling prophecy. Moreover, it is hard to keep Leech-Wilkinson's critique of performance practice from becoming a rejection of the music being performed although that is clearly not his intention. What seems to me to be the most dangerous aspect of proclaiming any aspect of culture as irrelevant, particularly in view of the present highly commodified cost-conscious culture, is the license to discard things. If indeed something is irrelevant, it is useless and can be discarded in favor of worthier pursuits, with important implications for governmental arts funding. This attitude makes me wonder about the value of a sustained polemic which nevertheless also serves to underline the relevance of Western art music precisely as it is customarily performed and recorded. After all, an insignificant target does not attract such fervent detractors.

My curiosity is piqued when parallels are drawn with other arts. Would there ever be a case for experts in their respective fields attacking the placement of paintings in museums, or the importance of protecting archeological sites so that the public can view them? The answer is premised on the importance of culture and personal meaning. As Kramer asserts (2005: 63), there is no room for complacency or neutrality, but the endorsement of specific ideologies is still a choice. Ian Pace (2020) stated this position in even more emphatic terms, ascribing to certain musicologists a fear of the very possibility that art's value can derive from attributes such as "opening up new realms of consciousness, sensation, [and] emotion beyond [those] narrowly circumscribed by moral philosophy or political dogma." Indeed, far from resembling a museum artifact, classical music does not solely command the attention of a handful of experts with an interest in conserving its history and practices although it may feel like this for specific niche areas (especially for music before 1700). Classical music as a whole, from medieval to contemporary, continues to provide emotional and intellectual outlets for its listeners, offering vistas of European culture across time and renegotiating and renewing its meaning every time its sounds bounce off both modern and historical cultural spaces. The value of classical music's contribution is not a function of its popularity.

In these exceedingly difficult times of the world in lockdown, people have experienced the paradox of coming together in isolation. Culture, both as an act of bringing people together and as a communication between artist and online audience, has never been more present or more pertinent in fulfilling its key role to help maintain our sense of humanity and, by extension, our collective mental health.

Leonidas Kavakos is a prominent Greek violinist, the recipient of prestigious awards such as the 2017 Léonie Sonning Music Prize. His latest contribution was an all-Bach recital for the celebration of the 65th anniversary of the Athens Festival, broadcast from the Ancient Greek theater of Epidaurus (July 13, 2020). This event followed a stream of important recordings on Decca and Sony Classical (2013–19) of works by Beethoven and Brahms. In his Easter message in the Greek media (2020), Kavakos echoed sentiments similar to those I have expressed here about the function and relevance of classical music in modern life. For Kavakos, the previous forms of normality saw the isolation of the modern citizen in an increasingly fast-paced, anxious, noisy, urban landscape with a narrow focus on the utilitarian aspects of living. This condition obscured from view the basic human needs for more meaningful communication and a sense of belonging to a community. And Kavakos goes even further, discussing cultural heritage and memory as the basis for getting closer to an ideal, pure conception of humanity.

Above all, the mirror mirrors the one who casts the reflection. When musicologists engage critically with a work or body of work, they also become objects of the critique and its conclusions. As Hans-Georg Gadamer (2013: 139) claimed long ago, underlining the researcher's bias is indispensable to understanding the work as a mirror that renews its meaning every time it is considered at both the individual and the societal levels, thus ultimately ensuring and renewing its relevance. In other words, a musical work renews its relevancy every time it is considered even if by its detractors. Ultimately, it renews its relevancy even when engaging with an audience unversed in its idiom or restricted to accessing its mere surface. And sometimes, the only form to express one's connectedness in today's fragmented society is music.

I will end with an apt and poetic quote from Kramer's "Three Variations on The Ruins of Athens" (2005: 62):

> A music that openly ponders both its relationship to representation and the generic value of its instrumental groupings is a music openly in search of the proper form to convey its own spirit. [...] That form is neither physical nor corporeal [...]. The proper form is acoustic.

References

About Classic FM. 2021. https://www.classicfm.com/about-classic-fm/values-history/. Accessed February 26, 2021.

Barth, G. 1992. *The Pianist as Orator: Beethoven and the Transformation of Keyboard Style*. Ithaca and London: Cornell University Press.

Cook, N. 2014. *Beyond the Score: Music as Performance*. Oxford: Oxford University Press.

Cooper, B. 2000. *Beethoven*. Oxford: Oxford University Press.

Fabian, D. 2015. *A Musicology of Performance: Theory and Method Based on Bach's Solos for Violin*. New edition [online]. Cambridge: Open Book Publishers, Available at: http://books.openedition.org/obp/1852. Accessed September 22, 2020.

Forster, E. M. 1910. *Howard's End*. https://www.gutenberg.org/files/2946/2946-h/2946-h.htm.

Gadamer H.-G. 2013. *Truth and Method*. London, New Delhi, New York, Sydney: Bloomsbury Academic.

Haynes, B. 2007. *The End of Early Music: A Period Performer's History of Music for the Twenty-First Century*. New York: Oxford University Press.

Kavakos, L. 2020. "I Ellada Edrase Topothetontas sto Kentro ton Anthropo." Kathimerini Gr. Available at: https://www.kathimerini.gr/1074649/article/epikairothta/ellada/h-ellada-edrase-topo8etwntas-sto-kentro-ton-an8rwpo. Accessed April 20, 2020.

Kivy, P. 1995. *Authenticities: Philosophical Reflections on the Musical Performance*. Ithaca and London: Cornell University Press.

Kramer, L. 1979. "Critical Response: The Shape of Post-Classical Music." *Critical Inquiry* 6 (1): 144–152.

--------1984. *Music and Poetry: The Nineteenth Century and After*. Berkeley and London: University of California Press.

--------2005. "Music, Historical Knowledge, and Critical Inquiry: Three Variations on The Ruins of Athens." *Critical Inquiry* 32(1): pp. 61–76. Available at: https://www.jstor.org/stable/10.1086/498004. Accessed May 15, 2020. Expanded in Kramer, L. 2010. *Interpreting Music*. Berkeley and London: University of California Press: 96–112.

Leech-Wilkinson, D. 2009. *The Changing Sound of Music: Approaches to Studying Recorded Musical Performance*. London: CHARM Available at: http://www.charm.kcl.ac.uk/about/about_structure. Accessed March 15, 2020.

--------2020. *Challenging Performance: Classical Music Performance Norms and How to Escape Them*. Available at: https://challengingperformance.com/the-book/. Accessed March 18, 2020.

--------2020a. "Of course not. Because classical music . . . " Twitter, March 20, 2020.

Muxfeldt, K. 2011. *Vanishing Sensibilities: Schubert, Beethoven, Schumann*. Oxford: Oxford University Press. Available at: DOI:10.1093/acprof:oso/9780199782420.001.0001. Accessed September 25, 2020.

Oliver, D. 2020. "A bizarre comment." Twitter, March 21, 2020.

Pace, I. 2013. "Hierarchies in New Music: Composers, Performers, and Works." *Desiring Progress Blog*. Available at: https://ianpace.wordpress.com/2013/09/29/hierarchies-in-new-music-composers-performers-and-works/. Accessed November 8, 2019.

--------2017. "The New State of Play in Performance Studies." *Music and Letters* 98 (2). Available at: https://doi.org/10.1093/ml/gcx040. Accessed April 10, 2020.

--------2020. "Classical Music Performance: Meaning and Relevance in Modern Society." *Desiring Progress Blog*. Available at: https://ianpace.wordpress.com/2020/08/23/my-contribution-to-the-debate-on-classical-music-performance-meaning-and-relevance-in-modern-society/?fbclid=IwAR0KB9Xtf7rAxo8bBeTFTO_5onuOY5wonqvUZCDqcNeMii5X_grfOnw8vP. Accessed August 23, 2020.

Subotnik, R. 1979. "Tonality, Autonomy, and Competence in Post-Classical Music." *Critical Inquiry* 6(1): 153–163. Available at: http://www.jstor.org/stable/1343093. Accessed March 25, 2020.

Tovey, D. F. 1935. *Essays in Musical Analysis: Symphonies and Other Orchestral Works*. London: Oxford University Press.

Chapter 6

A call for context:
historical explanations for our
disappearing classical music culture

Amy Damron Kyle

Sorbonne University

Abstract

The paper discusses how classical music suffered contradictions and limitations and argues that, just as we owe our definition of what classical music is and isn't largely to a musical canon formed in the late nineteenth century, classical music is not seen as a living and changing art form. School curriculum, instrument method books, music education, and even concert program notes often replicate the male-centered canon developed in a distant past, the paper contends. Yet, classical music may itself offer a recognition of the biased philosophy surrounding the musical canon and inspire a quest for a broader context of music's rich and diverse history.

Keywords: women's history, 19th-century music, philosophy, context, feminism

* * *

Questioning the vital signs of classical music is not a cold and detached inquiry. The question comes from the very community of musicians and musicologists who believe in its worth and are deeply invested in promoting and proving its relevance. Why then, in spite of the music that still resonates in concert halls, has cultural significance of classical music seemed to fade in the eyes of the general public? Perhaps this question can be answered in part by examining which composers' music is selected for performance, and what outdated cultural ideals inform this selection. In this investigation, perhaps there lies a means to re-awaken and revive classical music's role in contemporary society.

In 2018, the gender gap between performances of music by male and female composers in 89 of the largest symphony orchestras in the United States was enormous: 98.3% male to 1.7% female. Of the most performed composers the top three are still Beethoven, Mozart, and Brahms (Kijas, 2018). Recordings of the Year awarded by Gramophone from 1977 to 2017 haven't changed much either; not a single winning recording features a contemporary or historical female composer (Jolly, 2017: 1–31). This appears to say that the classical music world has not followed the social evolution of the last half-century. It is no surprise, then, that this genre is struggling to stay relevant. Wrangling connection with newer generations is the question of the day. But can audiences really still be expected to accept an art form where the male standard is presented as the only standard? In 2020 we've seen social movements that reflect a mounting cultural desire for inclusivity and for the understanding of previously marginalized groups. Yet in classical music, women composers still occupy a tiny portion of public stage time, at least in the symphonic sphere, though it is hard to imagine that the ratio is much different with chamber music; the male standard is still handed to the public as gender-neutral. The study of music is still mostly divided into *mainstream* music history, followed distantly by *women* in music. This distinction forms a barrier between the present and the past, and propagates social norms and values that have long since been abandoned.

Deeper historical investigation reveals a different context. For example, artists like Pauline Viardot-Garcia were at the center of the musical milieu of France and Europe for much of the nineteenth century. Admirers of her music, her colleagues, were names we all recognize: Saint-Saëns, Gounod, Massenet, Liszt, Berlioz, and many more. Yet her name, and those of other women like her, such as Louise Farrenc, Augusta Holmes, and Fanny Mendelssohn, are nowhere to be found in the present canon. A look at the standard canon, *with* the backdrop of historical context that includes women's achievements, reveals that it is neither reflective of the social norms of our day nor the true historical context of the time it venerates. Nor is a simple separation of professional and private spheres indicative of women's influence, or lack thereof. Adrianna Paliyenko's words regarding the history of French poetry translate easily to the history of music: "Women's absence, like their presence, shapes understanding of the French poetic past" (2016: 48). An understanding of the way in which the canon stays the same, and the way in which composers were admitted to it, allows for change and growth. Classical music *can* reach a public hungry for diversity by adding much-needed relevance and relatability through inclusive context. There is, then, much more to be said on how and why the musical canon dictates the endowment of the titles "great composer" or "musical genius." The present concept of genius is still formed using nineteenth-century philosophical and social values. Marjorie Garber describes how society still forms its ideal: "The genius was, and to some extent continues to be, the Romantic hero, the loner, the eccentric, the apotheosis of the individual...We prefer the myth" (Garber, 2012: 125).

Given only these touchstones, steeped as they are in ideals of masculinity, finding female musical geniuses past or present could be a challenge. As Vaughan Schmutz and Alison Faupel observe:

> The exclusion of women from Victorian literature and Viennese music had longstanding consequences for the gendered distribution of cultural legitimacy and consecration as it limited opportunities for female writers and musicians and diminished the likelihood that they would be included in the canons of their respective fields (2010: 688).

Though literary women of the nineteenth century did enjoy more visibility and success than their predecessors, the expectation of abandoning creative pursuits following marriage, still a social imperative for women, made great achievements intensely difficult. Women of talent were recognized *in spite of* their gender. Even Elisabeth Barrett Browning, in praise of George Sand, wrote that the peak of her creativity would come after death, having been freed from her gender (Paliyenko, 2016: 19):

> We see they woman-heart beat evermore
> Through the large flame. Beat purer, heart, and higher,
> Till God unsex thee on the heavenly shore,
> Where unincarnate spirits purely aspire!

One may be able to list a few literary women whose names have endured, but that does not change the fact that these women were viewed as the exception to the gender rule. Exceptional creativity was socially accepted as a male domain, even for the creative women who challenged the expectation.

With the growing market for printed music and the freelance culture of composition, ideals of originality as well as solitary creation took hold in the nineteenth century (Bracha, 2008: 209). Collaborators, often women, lost any chance at authorial status or recognition. This loss of collaborative credit for creations further closed the door to cultural acknowledgement of women's influence and contributions to the musical creations of others. Marketing concerts relied increasingly on a composer's persona during this time, relying heavily on the idea of the "lone male genius" (Citron, 1993: 179). Loss of acknowledgement of female creativity in the creation of great works, such as operas, to which women contributed, was a sign of the growing male-centered aesthetic of musical creation. The musical canon, lacking a collective context, was based on criteria of solitary masculine effort, then judged and affirmed by the same small group of male critics and historians. It is that continued lack of context which perpetuates and prolongs the myth that women had little influence on musical developments and styles.

Some may suggest that the age of musical geniuses is so problematic that it is best abandoned. But would rejecting the term *genius* accelerate the welcoming of exceptional female composers into our historical memory? Shall we take away the highest honor, which will certainly remain for those already established in the canon, at a time when women are finally beginning to receive some of their due for great works created? The canon and its accolades need not be erased, but should be modified. How do we remedy the unbalanced memory of men's and women's creations? How do we allow for "great" works, which have been judged so based on a structure accessible only to men, to continue to be great while making room in the mainstream for women's compositions? Does the admittance of the latter harm the accepted canon? I do not believe so. An evaluation of the criteria inherited from the nineteenth century is a critical step in opening the path towards a more inclusive canon and a clearer view of musical genius.

How is genius gendered?

Compositional choices require the lens of historical context: educational limitations, gender expectations, and the social implications of manifesting great talent within one's gender. An ambitious woman of any time period, but markedly during the nineteenth century, had a choice to make if her ambition was to write music. Did she "compose like a man," denying her own gender, but giving more freedom to her creative abilities, or did she "compose like a woman" and bend to the aesthetic expectations of her gender? There was no way for women to compose from a place of neutrality as male composers did. Ask any non-musician to name two female composers, and the evidence is clear. Perhaps within the musicological milieu there has been a slight paradigm shift, but the musical classroom for the general public still echoes the beliefs of the nineteenth century.

To further complicate the matter, music is often perceived as an art that *transcends* rather than reflects the social norms of its time. This paradigm further emphasizes and validates historically male-centered value criteria— such as the size of the work, stylistic breaks with the past, and professional critical reception—as neutral expectations (Citron, 1993: 224). The perceived neutrality of these benchmarks makes the canon rigid and hard to change. Our cultural acceptance of this nearsighted aesthetic stems from philosophical evaluations formed over centuries that culminated in the nineteenth century

(Young, 2014: 49). These philosophies inform the boundaries of our present-day canon and our judgements on exceptional creative talent.

Nineteenth-century philosophies: an inheritance

Edward Lowinsky traced the use of the term *genius* or its definition referring to a composer back to the Renaissance. Giovanni Spataro's letter in 1529 to a Venetian musician acknowledges the definition of musical "genius" by stating that written rules teach counterpoint, but good composers, like good poets, are simply born (Lowinsky, 1964b: 481). This idea that genius is born, not made, is a subtle acknowledgement that individuals have little control over their own possibility of creating great works if they are not born with the right characteristics. What chance, then, do women have if these characteristics refer to gender? From this time on, letters and published writing by prominent figures in history regularly praise and seek to identify compositional genius.

With the emergence of the concept, theories on who had the right to unbridled human imagination in music, and who did it best, were codified by prominent music theorists and philosophers. The process started in the early eighteenth century. Jean Philippe Rameau (1683–1764) and Jean Jacques Rousseau (1712–1778) helped solidify our understanding of the musical genius as both rule maker and rule breaker. Everyone else fell into the category of a skilled artist. The skilled artist must follow the rules, *not* break them—not having the heightened aesthetic sensibility to do so (Lowinsky, 1964a: 339). The concept of the genius as a rule-breaker was built around the image of composers like Beethoven, whom critics like Castil-Blaze, Joseph d'Ortigue, and Hector Berlioz (Schrade, 1943: 36) held up as their paragon. Unconsciously highlighting the difficulty women face in being recognized as exceptional in this social ambiance, Lowinsky states: "As it becomes permissible for the genius to break rules of art, so it becomes more or less acceptable that he as a person, transcend the norms of ordinary social behavior" (Lowinsky, 1964b: 487).

Obviously women were historically held to different expectations than men on what rules they would be allowed to break. Considering that gifted composing women were seen as skilled workers, not as geniuses, crossing the barrier of both social expectations as well as stylistic ones took on a very different significance for them. Can reactions to creations within social limits be viewed in another way? Could the audacious choice of composing great works as a woman, against the social norms of the day, be enough? Could the composer who never had access to training in orchestration still be a genius? Could small forms with less drastic stylistic breaks from the past (on the surface at least!) act as signs of exceptionality? For example, could Cecile Chaminade's Piano Sonata Op. 21, with its subversion of the normal balance between an aggressive first and submissive second theme and its denial of a tonal "other" be the stylistic break and the flash of genius that history has been missing (Citron, 1993: 153)? Could Pauline Viardot-Garcia's intriguing use of meter, combined with masterful compositional technique, to show feminine power in her chamber opera *Le Dernier Sorcier* open the door to a new look at genius (Kyle, 2019)? Given the prevailing norm of the genius as male rule-breaker, these women's professional trajectories, having broken the social rules through their gender, cannot be expected to be the same as that of their male peers. One must look carefully at the more subtle signs that merit attention. Perhaps historical female composers' understanding of their own social context should not be underestimated. Perhaps, without access to professional status, musical creation didn't produce the same anxiety of authorship for women, who thus produced works that took a different shape. This creative audacity and social awareness should be part of the broader context that reshapes the canon.

Female creatives and philosophy

In their article about French women opera composers, Letztler and Adelson point out that the French Revolution "brought an unprecedented level of female participation in public debate" (2000: 89), which contributed to a backlash against creative women that was simultaneously philosophical, physiological, and sexual. The critic Charles Maurras (1868–1952) equated women's genius with chaotic degeneration, a theft of the rights of the male gender, and the over sensualizing of art (Paliyenko, 2016: 55). Pierre-Joseph Proudhon went further by saying (my translation): "Genius, then, is the virility of mind, its abstract power, of generalization, of invention, of conception, hence the child, the eunuch, and the woman are left wanting" (Ibid: 32).

Exceptional women were seen as such an anomaly that Diderot, for one, referred to his intellectual correspondent Sophie Volland as a "man" (Parker, 1986: 98). In the next century, Jules and Edmond de Goncourt surmised that George Sand, Germaine de Staël, and Pauline Viardot-Garcia were actually hermaphrodites (Paliyenko, 2016: 36). And Julien Joseph Virey wrote (my tr.):

> If there exists a physical principle in the universe that can impart the whole capacity of expansiveness and daring to our intelligence, it is the sperm without a doubt the new *impetum faciens;* a source of vital vigor. By it, genius is illuminated … all the fine arts are lit by this torch of life (Ibid: 11).

From the de Goncourts to Virey we can see that the prevailing philosophy of male creative power, both literal and figurative, rendered women's creations simply not viable. Women, therefore, were essentially barred from the musical canons of the nineteenth century because their bodies were not men's bodies. This physiological inaccessibility to an all-male canon was compounded by the grant of universality given to those entrants who met the lone-male-composer ideal.

Limitations and redemptions of the canon

In this context, the creative process is neither important nor seen as the necessary basis for strokes of genius. Masterworks become the sole product of the celebrity-artist. This myopic view further leads to the mystique and unapproachability of the all-male genius.

Establishing the idealized image of members of this all-male canon as exemplary symbols further sanctifies the present musical canon and blinds the observer to the underlying bias that informed its formation. Thus, the canon is not seen for what it was: an elastic result of social values that change. The persona of the "lone male genius" is reinforced, and the canon continues to alienate new and unknown works.

Context can rehabilitate the title of genius through understanding its pathway, and can thus open it up to marginalized composers. Viewing the creative process as collaborative provides a new way of looking at established works, and reintroduces female composers and collaborators into the historical creative arena. For example, Hector Berlioz edited the definitive version of Gluck's *Orphée* side by side with Pauline Viardot-Garcia. Her contributions are well documented (Stier, 2011: 3). Renaming this version the Berlioz/Viardot edition has already begun, which opens the door to more historical context. Once women are seen as part of the musical world of their time, viewing their works in the context of influence becomes less challenging. Changing the focus of the historical paradigm from solitary agency to the activity of social groups provides the frame of reference needed to see how works of genius were actually created. It opens the historical landscape to view men and women writing and sharing their works side by side, though in different venues. Women like Pauline Viardot-Garcia were not at the periphery of the creative milieu of their day; they were at its heart. Context brought to bear on the lives of established great composers as well as of forgotten ones adds a layer of complexity, introduces multiple authorship, and normalizes the enjoyment and understanding of women's compositions.

Taking account of historical context means opening up the understanding of a work's reception to the impact of its social provenance. The path to the future must also include recovering documents of historical reception that do not exclude women or gloss over their work in the gendered terms often found in unpublished critical reviews. Valuation should be complicated, and its complexity must be acknowledged. Looking past public critical views to other written records of reception allows for value to be seen in women's works as well (Citron: 206). Using letters, unpublished journals, and memoirs, for example, not only gives insight into the genius manifested by female composers, but also gives us first-person accounts by the auditors of their works, bringing them from the periphery to the inner circle of creation.

The reception of Viardot-Garcia's compositions by both her male and female contemporaries is an example of genuine historical context in contrast to our *perception* of the terms on which the works of nineteenth-century women were received. Viardot's success and influence was subject to social prejudice and slowly erased over time by those that recorded our music history.

Pauline Viardot-Garcia's accomplishments and works were hailed during her lifetime (1821–1910) as those of a great artist. Liszt praised her as the first female composer of genius he had ever known. He wrote that her works contained "so much skill in harmonic subtleties (which would be envied by many famous composers)" (Liszt, 1881: 126). Clara Wieck Schumann said of her friend that she was "the most talented woman" that she had ever known (Jesesnsky, 2011: 268). Adolphe Adam described her as one who "sings in, and speaks five languages, who plays the piano like an angel, is as good a harmonist as anyone, who sings like her sister, and who composes things that we would have been proud to have written" (Fitzlyon, 1964: 75).

Perhaps society has vanquished the idea that a certain set of genitalia opens the door to possible creative genius. But in a time when Beethoven and Mozart still appear instantly in the mind of most of the public for classical music, ignorance of the substantial array of musical creations by gifted women composers is still the norm. But gender parity in programing is still viewed as a financial risk to most large symphony orchestras, especially in the United States. Why? Because the philosophies of the nineteenth century may seem outdated, but their influence is far from gone. The canon still presents the gold standard, and there are few public rewards in programming anything outside that accepted male-dominant standard. In their article reviewing revenue sources and concert programming of U.S. symphony orchestras, Pompe, Tamburri, and Munn describe the difficulty orchestras face in programming unfamiliar music such as music by female composers because their ticket sales drop when performing unfamiliar works by as much as 20%. They state: "There is evidence that SOs have an affinity for a small number of composers from classical and romantic periods which are representative of the standard repertoire" (Pompe, Tamburri, and Munn, 2011: 169–170). The canon not only tells an audience what they should like from their first experiences in the musical classroom (Bond, 2017: 154), but whom they should pay to hear. This is done without revealing its implicit biases.

Understanding the depth of the meaning of musical genius that we have inherited from nineteenth-century aesthetics can serve us now in our strivings for inclusion, for a richer comprehension of women's musical creations, then and now. Musical genius is part of how the musical story is told, and with deeper, more meaningful context that story can continue to evolve along with the social needs of our time. Revising historical context to include great female composers can inspire future generations, and engender a better understanding of how great music is made and who the "great composers" really were and are. By questioning the criteria built into the current canon, a culture of curiosity can be championed in the musical classroom and the concert hall. Curiosity invites an audience that includes the newest generations to participate in discovery and evaluation. Modification of the canon does not exclude already accepted great works, but merely brings great women into focus, into the concert hall, and into the ears of a generation longing for equality.

References

Bond, V. L. 2017. "Culturally Responsive Education in Music Education." *Contributions to Music Education* 42: 153–180.

Bracha, O. 2008. "The Ideology of Authorship Revisited: Authors, Markets, and Liberal Values in Early American Copyright." *The Yale Law Journal* 118: 186–271.

Citron, M. 1993. *Gender and the Musical Canon.* New Edition. Chicago: University of Illinois Press.

Fitzlyon, A. 1964. *The Price of Genius: A Life of Pauline Viardot.* London: John Calder.

Garber, M. 2012. *Loaded Words.* New York: Fordham University Press.

Jesesnsky, K. LaPorta. 2011. "The Life of Pauline Viardot: Her Influence on the Musicians of Nineteenth Century Europe." *Journal of Singing* 67(3): 267–275

Jolly, J. 2017. *The World's Best Classical Music Reviews: Celebrating 40 years of Gramophone Classical Music Awards.* London, MA: Music. Gramophone [Online, available at: https://reader.exacteditions.com/issues/61391/page/3]

Kijas, A. 2018. "What does the data tell us?: Representation, Canon, and Music Encoding." May 24 [online] Available at: https://medium.com/@kijas/ https-medium-com-kijas-what-does-the-data-tell-us-926ba830702f. Keynote delivered at the Music Encoding Conference University of Maryland, May 24, 2018.

Kyle, A. 2019. "The tale of two queens: flipping the script on the 'princess culture' in opera." December 5 [online] Available at: https://theconversation.com/profiles/amy-lorette-damron-kyle-722109/articles.

Letzter, J. and R. Adelson. 2000. "French Women Opera Composers and the Aesthetics of Rousseau." *Feminist Studies* 26(1): 69–100.

Liszt, F. 1881. "Pauline Viardot-Garcia." *Gesammelte Schriften*. Vol. 3, Leipzig: Kessinger Publishing.

Lowinsky, E. 1964a. "Musical Genius – Evolution and Origins of a Concept." *The Musical Quarterly* 50(3): 321-340.

--------1964b. "Musical Genius – Evolution and Origins of a Concept II." *The Musical Quarterly* 50(4): 476–495.

Paliyenko, A. 2016. *Genius Envy; Women Shaping French Poetic History 1801- 1900.* University Park, PA: The Pennsylvania State University Press.

Parker, A. 1986. "Did/Erotica: Diderot's Contribution to the History of Sexuality." *Diderot Studies* 22: 89-106.

Pompe, J., L. Tamburri and J. Munn. 2011. "Factors that influence programming decisions of US symphony orchestras." *Journal of Cultural Economics* 35(3): 167–184.

Schmutz, V. and A. Faupel. 2010. "Gender and Cultural Consecration in Popular Music." *Social Forces* 89(2): 685–707.

Schrade, L. 1943. *Beethoven in France: The Growth of an idea.* Oxford: Oxford University Press.

Stier, M. 2011. "The Power of Gluck and of his Interpreter: Pauline Viardot's part in the British Gluck Revival." *British Postgraduate Musicology* 11 (2011). http://britishpostgraduatemusicology.org/bpm11/. Accessed February 26, 2021.

Young, J. O. 2014. "On the Enshrinement of Musical Genius." *International Review of the Aesthetics and Sociology of Music* 45(1): 47–62.

Chapter 7

"The hard problem": classical music and the history of consciousness

Lawrence Kramer

Fordham University

Abstract

This essay derives from the keynote speech given at the 3rd AEMC Conference on Music, Communication and Performance. It examines the place of classical music in the history of consciousness—a history now changing rapidly. It shows how, in the pressure of the events that have recently pushed classical music into a corner, this art form finally appears for what it is: not the culturally authoritative form of music, but one addressed to a historically delimited audience absorbed by questions of subjectivity and its social repercussions. The paper argues that the question to ask ourselves is not whether classical music rises or falls, but what it is, and thus what we affirm if we continue to value it.

Keywords: classical music, history of consciousness, the hard problem, music and language, ontology of music

* * *

What does it mean in 2020 to ask about the fate of classical music? Is it a question about whether the music is an endangered species, or who its audience is and will be, or of its use on various media platforms, or of its standing in a rivalry with something called popular music? In any of these forms, the question seems to be prompted by the loss of a broad cultural authority that classical music once enjoyed. But in some ways that loss is illusory. For one thing, there is no such thing as "popular music" as opposed to music that is popular in the sense of being widely liked. Instead, there is a multitude of musical types, each with its own niche and its own mythology. For another thing, this fragmentation of the musical world, largely produced by digitally powered media platforms, means that no type of music can aspire to broad cultural authority as opposed to commercial success. The category of preeminent authority no longer exists as a prize to be won by music or anything else. We live in a condition of irreducible plurality that renders many old categories obsolete. The trouble is that the categories continue to be used as if unaware that they have become useless. The contemporary norm is multiplicity and coexistence—in other words, the absence of a norm. It is an understatement to say that we have not yet learned how to live with this condition, and not, of course, just in the arts. The social dilemmas that cling to classical music are not part of my topic here, but I will return to them at the end.

In 2020, the question about classical music needs to be asked differently: not whether this music rises or falls, but what it *is*, and thus what we would do, what we would affirm, if we continue to value it. In a curious way, however, the question is not about music. As I will shortly propose, it is about consciousness. For that reason, the answer is emphatically not to be based on musical form in the sense of design. The design of individual pieces of classical music, or any music, may be admirable or not, but the question concerns the category, not its instances. Although the answer may be illustrated at the level of the individual piece, the question is located at the level of the type, the level of form in the sense in which we speak of the novel as a form, or could once speak of cinema as a form. This is form in the further sense of what Wittgenstein (1954) called *Lebensform*, form of life: the array of values, dispositions, and even of worldviews that define the experience of this music. Like what the music is, the form of life that constitutes it depends on general practices, not their specific instances. The question thus cannot be answered simply by asking people what they value about the music. It is what they *do* by valuing it, not what they may or may not say about it, or know about it, that is at issue. Put more strongly, the issue is what valuing the music necessarily affirms regardless of what one might say or not say, know or not know about it.

For historical reasons, this issue begins with the problem of subjectivity—the chief matter of concern for most Western music since the mid-eighteenth century. In *Why Classical Music Still Matters* (2007), I proposed that to embrace classical music was to embrace, even if only nostalgically, a certain type of subjectivity born, or at least first fully recognized, in that era, together with the practices of attention meant to sustain it. I stand by that description, but I now want to take things considerably further—to give an account of the music based not on its formal characteristics, but on its mode of being. It is this last, ontological dimension, through which we can best pose the question of the music's value: to clarify what valuing it entails regardless of whether we keep it or lose it. But of course, I hope that the clarification can support the effort to keep it.

* * *

Because most classical music is fully composed, it draws attention away from the occasion of performance to the idea, which is also an ideal, of the composition. This can lead to unfortunate critical gushing over masterpieces (though that is no worse than wild-eyed fandom in other genres), but it can also lead to the individualization of the music as a part of the listener's personal repertoire of prized objects, points of orientation that give sense to the world. Classical music invites a certain concentration and absorption that does not do well with distraction. The music calls attention not only to its expressive values, but also to the processes that produce them. It reflects on its expressive values in the act of expressing them. But it does not, for the most part, allow the difference between expression and reflection to divide them from each other. At least it tries not to. Naturally there are exceptions, but the default relationship between expression and reflection in classical music is a division that unites, the condition that Jean-Luc Nancy (2009: 121) calls *partage*: sharing, partaking, apportioning.

There are two obvious problems with this account that need to be addressed before we can proceed. The first is that there is no uniformity of practice in listening to classical music, or indeed any music. We can listen intently, or distractedly, or anything in between. The second problem is that the matter to which the music invites attention varies drastically in complexity and duration—the latter ranging from under a minute for a Chopin Prelude to more than a hundred minutes for Mahler's Third Symphony. So in talking about what I will call "classical listening," just what are we talking about? Are we being descriptive or prescriptive? And how can we tell the difference?

Classical listening is not, or should not be, the prescriptive practice that was often decreed during the twentieth century, but perhaps not often followed. Instead, like any listening practice, classical listening is the exercise of the habit of mind that its chosen music encourages. Its basis is not what to listen for, but how to listen intently. Classical listening represents the invention of a possibility. It forms an exemplary limit case that makes available a certain practice of attention and perception. Engaging in the practice is supposed to give both pleasure and knowledge. But this "supposed to" can at best be a promise. Making rules for listening has been nothing but bad for classical music. The question is not how you *should* listen, but how you *can*. Classical listening is not "structural listening." It does not depend on being instructed in the mysteries of musical form, but only on being attentive to the possibilities made available when one listens, so to speak, beyond just hearing, however pleasurable or exciting the hearing may be. Classical music is above all the music that encourages us to listen beyond just hearing. It is music in which expression is not only an end, but also a means to further ends—further pleasure, further knowledge. Listening to this music becomes oppressive the moment that it becomes normative. No one is likely to practice classical listening all the time. But if one practices it *some* of the time, if one is open to it as a part of a larger repertoire of practices of apprehension, the results can be revelatory. That, in any case, is the promise.

The rewards of classical music have many sources, from the simple enjoyment of melody and its transformations to admiration for virtuoso performance to the jolt of expressive meaning concentrated in numinous moments. But the feature of classical music that organizes and subsumes all the others is the event, taking "event" both in the general sense of significant occurrence and the recent philosophical sense of creative discontinuity, transformational change. The event consists of the arrival of a decisive change in any aspect of the musical experience. It registers as the strong sense that *something has happened.*

Classical music is defined by this event-character, this eventfulness. It is music that conveys the sense that something has happened, something is happening, as well as music in which something is expressed. Moreover, in contrast to improvised music, with classical music the event precedes the performance; the event can be reiterated from one performance to another— never exactly, of course, but exactly enough. This quality carries over to the listener who concentrates, who listens for what happens: listening for the event is eventful listening. The goal of classical listening is to give oneself over to the event.[1]

The character of the musical event depends historically on the separation of music from language, not in practice, but in concept. As long as music primarily meant vocal music, music could maintain a connection to the tradition of art as mimesis, the "regime of representation," as Jacques Ranciére calls it (2004: 12–15), which held sway from classical antiquity to the eighteenth century. When vocal music was the best example of the category of music—a best

---

[1] In *A Thousand Plateaus* (1988: 192-193), Deleuze and Guattari identify the literary genre of the novella with the question "What happened?" and oppose it to the tale, which asks "What will happen?" For classical music, the equivalent question would be "What has happened?" Classical music occupies the present perfect tense. The event embodied in the music is always still in progress; its course is never fully run, not even after the music is over. The listener is one in the midst; the question is: of what? As for the answer, it may take the form of a full interpretation in writing, but it may equally well occur on a smaller scale as a jotting or a remark spoken aloud or the stuff of a conversation. It may also arrive, and surely most often does, in compressed form, as a phrase, a description, a memory, a usage, a metaphor, a way of moving. The answer, in Deleuze and Guattari's terms, spins out along a line of flight.

example is an instance that dominates its category—music could borrow some of the representational character it did not have on its own. Instrumental music lacked words, but not its kinship with music linked to words. The different character of instrumental music was only a small problem. But the rise of the concept of the aesthetic in the eighteenth century marked the decline of the regime of representation. Imitation receded in favor of free-standing form even where imitation was present. In music it was mostly absent. New musical styles based more on internal diversity than on affective consistency made its absence more pronounced. By the end of the century, instrumental music was a big problem. It made both too much sense and too little. Too little, because its lack of words seemed like a lack of meaning. Too much, because it was nonetheless perfectly intelligible.

The lack of words in instrumental music had evolved, and with retroactive impact, from a contingent condition to a definitive one. The music maintained an affirmative lack in relation, not only to words in a simple literal sense, but also to the extended network of words and images—the imagetext—that constitutes the general order of representation in Western cultures. The absence of representation became part of the music's presence, even—to echo the case with imitation—when representation was present. The result, paradoxically, was to make music more available to the imagetext than ever before although this development became fully evident only with the rise of modern media, in the first instance cinema. In association with words or images, music, with unparalleled expressive fluidity, readily adapts itself to the structure of feeling behind what is said or seen. Its participation may be sympathetic, ironic, contrary, or mixed—perhaps most often mixed. The music both fits itself to the representation and changes the representation to fit itself. The same music can repeat this process with different representations, and different representations can have recourse to the same music.

When music is heard apart from the imagetext the result has always been easy to feel, but hard to describe. The instrumental genres suspend the use of music's expressive fluidity—render it inoperative as Giorgio Agamben (2015: 62–63, 277–279) might say—and refocus it on the music, the sounding event, as such. This remains true of vocal music heard in a concert setting; classical vocal music juxtaposes the music's expressive use with its suspension in favor of the instrumental event, and does not necessarily reconcile them. Historically, the result felt like a momentous discovery, and at the same time the realization of something waiting to happen. For J. G. Herder, writing in 1800, instrumental music represented the culmination of a long, slow history, but its rise had been latent from the beginning: "Orpheus moved Orcus with the language of his lyre; the Eumenides would never have yielded to a mortal's words" (le Huray and Day, 1988: 192, translation modified). Herder's Orpheus sings with his instrument, not with his voice. He is the first classical musician in more ways than one.

It is now a truism that in the later eighteenth-century European art music became independent of language, but what the truism means is that instrumental music became the best example of music. With classical music, the best example became unusually robust; it became definitive. To say what resulted from this change has perhaps been *the* aesthetic problem of classical music—a hard problem with a great many answers in contention. My own answers are well-enough known. They involve, at a minimum, the claims that detachment from the imagetext does not constitute a detachment from meaning, and that music's suspension of the imagetext does not cancel either the imagetext or music as sources of meaning for each other. My concern here, however, does not lead back to the hard problem of musical meaning, but forward to the relationship of classical music to an even harder problem, the so-called "hard problem" of consciousness.

The term "hard problem" was coined by the Australian philosopher David Chalmers (1995), and has passed into common use. It is the problem of how conscious sentience arises from purely material processes. At a minimum, such sentience extends to humans and a wide range of animals; some recent philosophers would extend it further, even to matter in general. But sentience is not the whole story. In *The Hum of the World* (2019: 210–220), I suggest that human consciousness is not an eternal verity, but a specific cognitive modality that may now have to share the stage with something else because of technological changes in the conditions of perception. If that is so, classical music becomes both important and elusive because of its high investment in consciousness. This investment takes two forms. The first we have already observed; it is concentration or intensity. The other is the genesis of self-awareness. What I will propose shortly is that classical music was devised to be the soft answer to the hard problem of consciousness as self-awareness. Or call it the *very* hard problem because its difficulties are not only matters of explanation, but also matters of experience.

* * *

The first-person narrator of Sebastian Faulks's novel *Where My Heart Used to Beat* (2015) recalls a conversation about "the curse of human self-awareness," which he concluded by exclaiming "I would trade all of Beethoven for the happy ignorance in which my pre-*sapiens* forbears lived. In that way I would still be a part of the natural world, and not an interloper marked with the brand of Cain" (133). The trope that opposes natural unselfconsciousness to the burden of consciousness has a long history, going back at least to Rousseau. But the narrator's version is extreme. It represents consciousness not just as unhappy, but as criminal. Self-awareness is somehow equivalent to Cain's murder of his brother. And the curse of self-awareness stems not from Cain's crime, but from the mark, the inscription, the writing, that recalls the crime. The mark is the curse. (A little earlier the narrator has said that natural selection did not require us "to write all of Mozart" [132]). It turns out that the narrator's invocation of Cain arises from his experience of combat in World War II; he is marked, scarred, by his memories of that trauma. To erase the mark, he would even be willing to repeat a form of Cain's crime and win obliviousness by trading someone away.

But why is that someone Beethoven? It's plain that the narrator is reaching for a big name, full of cultural capital; nothing less would make his point. But he could have mentioned Plato, or Michelangelo, or the default choice, Shakespeare, so why Beethoven? Why one of the preeminent representatives of classical instrumental music, supposedly the least conceptual of the high arts and therefore the least suitable to represent the height, or in this case, the intolerable depth, of human self-awareness?

The novel does not say, but one answer is implicit in the question. The name "Beethoven" represents the extended instrumental work as the paradigmatic form of classical music unlinked from text and voice (Mozart, we might imagine, gets left behind because he wrote so many operas). Suppose then that we grant the two assumptions implied by the narrator's choice of Beethoven. First, we assume that the music represented by Beethoven has little or no conceptual content. Second, we assume that this music nonetheless conveys the superlative degree of human self-awareness. There is only one way that both of these assumptions could be true. Both would apply if the music were to exemplify the process by which human self-awareness comes into being regardless of what the human subject becomes aware of.

This conclusion is consistent with the familiar old idea that music, taken purely in on its own terms, consists essentially of expression without content. For many years I have argued that this idea is mistaken. But there is no reason why music of this kind should not *both* represent the genesis of self-awareness regardless of content *and* convey by complex and indirect means a conceptual orientation that invites and repays interpretation in both language and performance. There is no reason why these processes should not be simultaneous; there is equally no reason why they should not be successive. It may even be that one cultural function of classical music is to embody the quality of meaningfulness in excess of anything the music might be thought to mean. Historically, that has been taken as a license not to think about its meaning, or to ask what its meaning might consist of. But again, there is no reason why this music should not *both* embed meaning *and* embody meaningfulness. The perception of one does not invalidate the perception of the other.

It is perfectly reasonable, then, to entertain the idea that in listening to a classical instrumental work we rehearse and re-inherit the condition of human self-awareness, and to ask what that might mean in any particular case. It would also be reasonable to suggest that to keep this music alive in our culture is to affirm our self-awareness as a value, brand of Cain or not.

Of course, any music might appeal to self-awareness, and some classical music does not. But no music can do everything, and not doing everything is no defect. The strong inclination of classical music to incorporate reflective distance, not apart from its immediacy, but as a part *of* it, does seem distinctive. We might even risk saying that classical music refuses to relinquish the otherness that much other music tries to overcome. It is never "all there" in the moment no matter how enthralling the moment might be. The question remains, however, of *why* classical music behaves this way.

To suggest an answer, I need to return to my observation that the concentrated listening practice encouraged by classical music was foundational for a historical type of subjectivity born of the European Enlightenment. One well-known feature of this subjectivity is that it is habitually self-reflective, self-reflective even to a fault. It is a subjectivity grounded in the experience of subjectivity itself. This circular movement does not prevent the conscious subject from correctly perceiving factual states of affairs, but it does mark a historical change in what it means to be conscious. One way to describe that change is to say that it installs a version of the hard problem at the center of conscious life. The subject discovers an internal obstacle to self-perception and self-understanding that consciousness is powerless to penetrate.

An important consequence is that even if we could solve the hard problem in David Chalmers's sense, it would do us no good. Individual consciousness cannot account for its own origins. As the American philosopher Judith Butler observes (2010), any account that one gives must assume in advance the consciousness it seeks to explain. To this we might add that any consciousness that seeks to give such an account must be self-aware, and that it can no more account for the origin of its self-awareness than it can for its simple sentience. Impossibility aside, as Butler also observes, we are asked to give accounts of ourselves all the time, and we do try to give them. But our every attempt is cut short by the very thing that makes it possible, namely language. We have little or no knowledge of our preverbal experience except insofar as we put it into words—words that necessarily presuppose whatever they are meant to explain. St. Augustine, one of the first people to make such an attempt, is immediately caught in the trap. In his *Confessions* (1955, I.vi.: 7–12), he recalls his infancy as a state of frustration and anger at his inability to communicate his desires to the adults who reared him because he did not understand the language they used to communicate with each other. It sounds reasonable. But how does he know? His description presupposes the understanding of language, intention, desire, adulthood, other minds, and so on, all of which could be possible only *after* Augustine had become a self-aware subject. What came before remains dark. This dilemma is the *really* hard problem.

Classical music was in part devised in response to it. The music did not represent a solution, but rather a means of making a solution seem unnecessary. In the eighteenth century, when the kinds of music and of listening that would later fall under the category of the "classical" began to be consolidated, the question of the origin of consciousness, and more, of self-aware subjectivity, was a major philosophical problem, equally compelling, for example, to the British empiricists and the German idealists. The classical instrumental composition offered an opportunity to trace the origin of self-awareness without the impediment of language. The opportunity did come at a cost; the loss of language was also a loss of specificity. But the music could and did convey the rise and imagine the fate of self-awareness. It did so in sensory rather than conceptual terms, and thus embraced as a mystery what language would have to accept as a perplexity. Because the music was intelligible independent of language, even when it incorporated language, it afforded the feeling that the listener was partaking in a self-awareness that could give an account of itself in the course of being heard. When Hegel in his *Aesthetics* (le Huray and Day, 1988: 237) said that "Subjective inner consciousness is the determining principle of music," and that instrumental music "is not determined by any hard and fast content and therefore…is allowed complete freedom in and for itself," he was summing up some 50 years of previous thought on the subject.[2] The feeling of subjectivity in action is based on an illusion, but an illusion that does not so much deceive the senses as extend them. The nearest analogy is probably to the moving image. The self-awareness heard in classical music is like the movement of bodies on screen. We know they are not alive, but cannot perceive them as other than lifelike. They have a life of their own.

To be clear, I am not saying that no other music can do this, or that classical music always does it, or does it to the same degree. The point, rather, is to recognize that a distinctive tendency exists, and that it is strong. If we agree with Faulks's narrator, we should avert our ears. If we don't, there's always Beethoven.

---

[2] See also, Bonds, 2014, Steinberg, 2004, and Kramer, 1995: 33-66.

* * *

This tendency of classical music carries an important implication. The kind of self-awareness that the music exemplifies is as much a historical phenomenon as the music is. Consciousness should not be confused with its basis in simple sentience. And consciousness, human consciousness—to return to the suggestion made in *The Hum of the World*—has a history. We may not be able to track its beginnings, but we can trace its genealogy, describe the means used to record it over time, and examine its relationships to communication and information technologies that both support and transform it. Accordingly, the question of the value and status of classical music is also the question of the value and status of consciousness, in the sense of the self-awareness of the conscious human being. We can perhaps recognize in retrospect that the value of the music, and its cultural function as well, rests with its power to be a repository of self-awareness that listeners can draw on if they choose.

Classical music developed to give self-reflective, but self-perplexed, consciousness a series of portraits with which to contend. It quickly recruited earlier music to the same end; as Mozart observed in 1783, "We love to entertain ourselves with every possible master, the old as well as the *modern*" (Leisinger, undated). By the turn of the nineteenth century, and symbolically linked to the career of Beethoven, the music increasingly comes to be regarded as something to be realized and interpreted, something to be reanimated in the passage of each performance from notation to sound.

Classical music especially seeks, or historically has sought, to be regarded this way. In recent years this ambition has met with disapproval from musicologists who regard it as coercive, and who certainly have a point in that the music was often *used* coercively. But to steal a phrase from one of the guilty parties, Theodor Adorno, the music needs to be defended from its admirers. The classical score is incomplete by design. The music extracted from it must be pieced together and projected as a kind of material utterance—not an object, or a fixed "work" to be idolized, but a "thing" in a quasi-Heideggerian sense, both something one lives with and makes use of and an imaginary form incised in time.[3] The music in this sense must be recognized as requiring not only repetition, but also understanding and interpretation in being repeated, and again in being remembered and described. The classical score is not meant to be obeyed; it is meant to be used.

But it is meant to be used with care. Classical music differs from most other kinds by asking for limited appropriation. There are no covers for classical

---

[3] See Heidegger, 2015: 161-184.

works—though of course there are arrangements and transcriptions. The classical score asks to be reproduced *both* with a high degree of exactitude *and* with a high degree of variability. Concert performers are usually expected to follow the score in essentials even if they make changes or adjustments in detail; they are supposed to recognize in the music a principle of resistance to the very appropriation that any performance necessarily seeks—and needs to find. In an important sense, this resistance just *is* the musical work, which is always virtual and never finished. The resistance is not there not to win, but to lose creatively.

* * *

It is now time to illustrate the arguments presented here with some actual music. To that end, I turn to music that has fascinated me before (2002), and that can stand as an especially strong best example because it not only retraces a course of self-awareness, but also reflects on its doing so. The secondary or higher-order reflection that more commonly remains implicit here breaks forth and enters into the musical action, and decisively at that.

The music is the fourth movement, the finale, of Schubert's Piano Trio No. 2 in E-flat (1827). It is a somewhat rambling movement, and a somewhat anxious one, characterized by a strong percussive emphasis in its melodies. But what is most distinctive about this finale is that it is interrupted twice by the main theme of the Trio's slow second movement, a brooding melody for cello partly derived from a Swedish folksong. These returns demand to be understood as meaningful events if only because they are unusual. For them to count as meaningful not much interpretation is required. It is perfectly possible to think of them simply as lyrical episodes that calm the tendency of the finale's own themes to agitation, even to violence. But even if we settle for that obvious description, it does not explain why the calming episodes have to be revivals of the earlier theme, which, incidentally, is not particularly calm.

So we have to go further. It is also possible to think of these melodic returns in much more sophisticated terms. One might, for example, hear them as calling up the *Volksgeist* against an anxious modernity heard in the finale's much-repeated shifts from its confident first theme to the percussive second one. More ambitiously, since there is no limit to the production of meaning, one might think of the cello theme, with its roots in song, as a symbolic form in which language has a residual presence. The solo cello stands in the place of the voice. The purely instrumental themes of the movement lack this dimension—a lack that would not matter if the movement were not so edgy. The cello theme would thus not merely bring calm, but bring calm specifically by invoking it with a surrogate word, a surrogate song, which the instrumental movement should not need to put its house in order, and yet does need. The movement has allowed itself too much freedom, in Hegel's view the inherent defect of instrumental music; it must be curbed. Going on from there, we might hear the returning melody as a sign drawn from the Lacanian symbolic order, the ruling order of language and law. The melody would be an utterance that can, but also must, be used to curtail the drive-based surplus of activity that sprawls through the finale, and thus to turn the sprawl into a coherent if surely a fictitious whole.

This ladder of meanings is important in its own terms. Its first and lowest rung implies all of the others, and more besides. But in relation to the hard problem the ladder of meanings is useless. Although it remains very relevant to a concrete understanding of the music, it has no impact on the music's underlying relationship to the genesis of self-awareness. The drama of that genesis is equally compatible with all of the many things those sounds must mean.

How do the cross-references between movements project that drama? Let me suggest three ways.

First, on the model of Beethoven's Fifth Symphony, the cross-references affirm the multi-movement composition as a single work, and not as a compact anthology of four separate works. In that respect they turn the Trio into a kind of manifesto on behalf of classical listening, which has not yet fully established itself as a practice in 1827. The music makes distraction a liability.

Second, the cross-references present recollection as a source of meaning. In particular they mobilize the capacity to recall distant events, to recover the past despite the elapsing of eventful time between then and now. It makes a difference that an entire movement intervenes between the introduction of the cello theme and its returns. The Trio thus posits that classical listening is a practice of memory as well as a practice of attention.

In so doing, the Trio makes an important departure from its model. Beethoven's symphony orients the listener toward the future by recalling the motto theme of the first movement at the start of the third, with half the symphony yet to come. Schubert's Trio orients the listener toward the past by recalling a bygone theme almost too late, when most of the music is over. The difference may be glossed as one of potentiality versus facticity, a distinction subject to a wide variety of realizations. But more important than any single one of these is the establishment of the dimension of questioning, in which memory and expectancy become contrary media of self-awareness. The memory in the Trio, moreover, is initially presented as if it were involuntary, something that occurs to one rather than something one retrieves. The bygone theme comes out of nowhere. The second appearance, however, is a purposeful retrieval; the music goes searching for it, and, having found it, replaces its gloomy accompaniment with a halo of lightness and delicacy. The pattern suggests the characteristic means by which memory passes from unawareness to raw awareness to self-awareness. In this respect the Trio also returns, in another act of memory, to its model since Beethoven reverses his future-orientation into a past-orientation when he recalls the mysterious transition from the symphony's third to its fourth movement in the midst of the latter.

The extended and intensified interplay between memory and expectancy that, the Trio tells us, is basic to classical instrumental music, temporarily alters the feeling of passing time. Held in the dimension of questioning, the music gives time a sensory presence and turns it into a tangible source of pleasure. All music surely does this to some extent. Classical music does it extensively.

Finally, the Trio, like the symphony, presents the appropriation of the past as a means of transformation or reconciliation. It presents self-awareness as the product of re-living the already lived. The basis of this transformative power is the combination of recollection with reinterpretation, such that the recollected matter changes in a consequential way. The movement travels from immediacy to self-awareness via a process of recollection that travels from literal recall to affirmative re-creation.

* * *

The sources of classical music's ability to do such things are historical, but they are also ontological; the categories blend into each other fairly quickly. The historical promptings are the post-Enlightenment establishment of pleasure as part of a legitimate social good, the pursuit of happiness, and the liberating potential of such pleasure with respect to older regimes of asceticism and worldly denial. Hegel echoes these tendencies when he leaps from the premise that instrumental music has no meaning determined by language to the conclusion that the music is therefore "allowed complete freedom in and for itself." The leap is illogical, but emotionally resonant. The true premise is the freedom. In particular it is the freedom of a consciousness made aware of itself through sound.

But of course, instrumental music has a long history, one that predates these concerns with subjectivity and self-awareness. What brought them together? One answer is the change that occurs when instead of thinking of instrumental music merely as music *without* language one thinks of it as music *free* of language. Apprehended in those terms, the music exemplifies a self-sufficiency that would not have been available earlier because it had not yet been thought of. It had not yet become a condition to be exemplified. Once the thought has been produced, everything changes. Calling such music self-sufficient—Hegel's term; others spoke of it as independent—is not a simple act of classification. It counts as what I have elsewhere termed a constructive description, a description that in part creates the reality of what it describes. Thinkers like Hegel were right, not because instrumental music "is" what they thought it to be, but because the language of their thought allowed the music to *become* what they thought it to be, or something like it.

This change was extended and diversified by new compositional styles, but it was not a change in compositional styles as such. It was a change in music's mode of being. No one could have foreseen how far-reaching the consequences would be. Regardless of whether such music is old or modern, regardless of whether it includes singing, its performance in real time now becomes a pageant of mind-like phenomena: affect, energy, process, sensation, signification, discourse, illocution, memory, agency—the list goes on. Music becomes the play of mind in the form of sound. That is what classical music can still offer us—if we're still interested.

* * *

But hold on. Just who is this "we" I have just invoked? I have been speaking as if the practices of attention and reflection encouraged by classical music were universally available, as well they should be—and of course are not. They are social privileges that *should* become rights for everyone, and if classical music is to matter in the way I have outlined here, our ways of presenting it, and talking and thinking about it, and *hearing* it, need to drop all pretensions to supremacy, especially white supremacy, and meet others on their own equal terms. We need to act on the premise that classical music is not inherently "elitist," whatever that much-abused term may mean.

My personal history with the music was anything but that. As a teenager in New York circa 1963, I got my musical education mainly by going to free concerts in the summer and borrowing LP records from the New York Public Library. There was no money for much else. And I'm not complaining about that; in fact, I loved it. The browsers in the library and the audiences at the concerts were not all wealthy and not all grey-haired and not all white, but they all loved this music. Well: that was all long ago and the moment, idealized in memory, is long lost. But I would still like to think that if classical music could matter that way then, it could still matter that way now.

References

Agamben, G. 2015. *The Use of Bodies*. Translated by A. Kotsko. Stanford: Stanford University Press.

Augustine. 1955. *Confessions*. Translated by A. Outler. Accessed September 22, 2020. https://www.ling.upenn.edu/courses/hum100/augustinconf.pdf.

Bonds, M. E. 2014. *Absolute Music: The History of an Idea*. Oxford: Oxford University Press.

Butler, J. 2010. *Giving an Account of Oneself.* New York: Fordham University Press.

Chalmers, D. 1995. "Facing up to the problem of consciousness." *Journal of Consciousness Studies* 2: 200–19.

Deleuze, G. and F. Guattari. 1988. *A Thousand Plateaus.* Translated by B. Massumi. Minneapolis: University of Minnesota Press.

Faulks, S. 2015. *Where My Heart Used to Beat.* New York: Henry Holt.

Heidegger, M. 1971. *Poetry Language Thought.* Translated by A. Hofstadter. New York: Harper Perennial.

Kramer, L. 2002. *Musical Meaning: Toward a Critical History.* Berkeley and London: University of California Press.

--------*The Hum of the World.* 2019. Berkeley and London: University of California Press.

--------*Why Classical Music Still Matters.* 2007. Berkeley and London: University of California Press.

Le Huray, P. and J. Day (eds.). 1988. *Music and Aesthetics in the Eighteenth and Eraly-Nineteenth Centuries.* Cambridge, UK: Cambridge University Press.

Leisinger, U., et al. Undated. *Mozart Briefe und Dokumente – Online Edition.* Salzburg: Internationale Stiftung Mozarteum, Bibliotheca Mozartiana. http://dme.mozarteum.at/DME/briefe/letter.php?mid=1302&cat. Accessed February 26, 2021.

Nancy, J.-L. 2009. *Dis-enclosure: The Deconstruction of Christianity.* Translated by B. Bergo, G. Malenfant, and M. B. Smith. New York: Fordham University Press.

Ranciére, J. 2004. *The Politics of Aesthetics: The Distribution of the Sensible.* London: Continuum.

Steinberg, M. 2004. *Listening to Reason: Culture, Subjectivity, and Nineteenth-Century Music.* Princeton: Princeton University Press.

Wittgenstein, L. 1954. *Philosophical Investigations.* Translated by G.E.M. Anscombe. London: Macmillan.

A Small Postscript:
Musical awakenings

I - Lawrence Kramer

Asked in 2020 by *The New York Times* to recommend five minutes that would make a listener love classical music, the soprano Julia Bullock chose "L'Indifferent" ("The Indifferent One"), the final song in Ravel's cycle *Shéhérazade*, composed in 1903. Bullock chose this song not simply because she admired it or thought it would be attractive, but because it was the source of her awakening to the power of classical music, and, further, through the music, to a new sense of self. The awakening was to an experience still to come, but the promise of which was already there in the music:

> My mouth fell open and tears welled in my eyes. I didn't know what she was singing about; I didn't know what harmonies were being played; I didn't know the composer, or the poet, or the content, but I knew that it was affecting my body and mind in ways that I had yet to experience. I was overwhelmed by the power matched with the ease. I was overwhelmed by the constant and extreme, yet seamless, shifts. I didn't understand what I was listening to, and I didn't need to, but it made me want to listen on, and on and on and on. This album was my introduction to classical music, and the brilliance of the human voice (Wang 2020).

Although these remarks emphasize the music and the voice rather than the lyric, there is, it so happens, an uncanny resonance between Bullock's experience and the poem set by Ravel: "L'indifferent," by "Tristan Klingsor" (Arthur Leclère). Here is the text in my English translation:

> Your eyes are tender as a girl's,
> Young stranger,
> And the delicate curve
> Of your beautiful face, shaded by down,
> Is even more alluring in its line.
> Your lips chant by my doorstep
> A language unknown and charming
> Like a music with wrong notes (une musique fausse).
> Come in! And let my wine bring you comfort ...
> But no, you pass by

And from my threshold I see you recede
Making a final graceful gesture
And your hips a little bent
By your feminine and weary gait.

(Oxford Lieder, 2021)

The text invites comment for the sexual ambiguity it brings to the theme of a chance encounter, but for present purposes its musical analogy is its most pertinent feature. Like the music he sings, the young stranger both allures and eludes the listener. His sexual duality parallels his essentially musical ability to satisfy and frustrate desire in the same action by departing as soon as he appears. It is possible to hear this poem, especially as set by Ravel, as a parable of musical awakening.

* * *

Bullock's remarks also resonate uncannily with a parallel awakening imagined in an American novel written almost 100 years ago. The power she heard in Ravel's music was something that she experienced newly, but it is not a new power, nor was it in 1925, when Ellen Glasgow's *Barren Ground* was published. The novel is generally acknowledged to be autobiographical, so the awakening here may be as much the author's as it is the character's:

> She sat in the concert hall waiting for the music to begin. At first she had tried to make out the names on the program, desisting presently because they confused her. Beethoven. Bach. Chopin. She went over the others again, stumbling because she could make nothing of the syllables. A-p-p-a-s-s-i-o-n-a-t-a. What did the strange word mean? P-a-t-h-é-tique—that she could dimly grasp.

> Suddenly, while she struggled over the letters, the music floated toward her from the cool twilight of the distance. This was not music, she thought in surprise, but the sound of a storm coming up through the tall pines at Old Farm. She had heard this singing melody a thousand times, on autumn afternoons, in the woods. Then, as it drew nearer, the harmony changed from sound into sensation; and from pure sensation, rippling in wave after wave like a river, it was merged and lost in her consciousness.

> In the beginning, while she sat there, rapt in startled apprehension, she thought of innumerable things she had forgotten; detached incidents, impressions which glittered sharply, edged with light, against the mosaic of her recollections…Suddenly she was pierced by a thousand

splinters of crystal sound. Little quivers of light ran over her. Beads of pain broke out on her forehead and her lips. She clenched her hands together, and forced her body back into her chair. "I've got to stand it. No matter what it does to me, I've got to stand it." (Glasgow, 1925).

Like Bullock, Glasgow's alter ego finds herself overwhelmed by the music; she starts from a point of unknowing that becomes the origin of fuller knowledge; she recognizes an as-yet unknown part of herself in the music; and she is changed by the experience. The chief difference is that the music carries the fictional listener to the point where pleasure turns to pain, but the difference is misleading: the pain in this case is as formative an experience as the pleasure. The music provides the resilience by which it is possible to withstand its shocks.

Glasgow's account literally—really literally—has her protagonist spelling out the significance of the experience the music will bring. The novel's readers are invited to fill out this dawning understanding by their own (presumed) prior knowledge of the music: to verify in their own experience what the character is discovering. Meanwhile the names of those two Beethoven sonatas symbolize the gamut that feeling, informed by such music, may run: from action to suffering, passion to pathos.

Among the vital signs still flourishing in classical music, the music's long-standing power to provoke self-discovery, something also reflected throughout this volume, may be one of the strongest. But self-discovery in the inward sense is only half the story. Selves are inescapably social, and any awakenings that classical music may bring, like any awakenings at all, bear on our place in the wider world. Glasgow's heroine quickly learns as much. The endurance she embraces after the concert enables her to assume a place of responsibility in a community she had abandoned: "Passion stirred again in her heart; but it was passion transfigured, recoiling from the personal to the impersonal object. It seemed to her, walking there in the blue twilight, that the music had released some imprisoned force in the depths of her being, and that this force was spreading out over the world, that it was growing wider and thinner until it covered all the desolate country at Old Farm." She thus takes on the burden of restoring life to the barren ground of the book's title.

And with that, I turn over the discussion of this vital topic to my fellow editor.

—

II - Alberto Nones

If the COVID-19 pandemic has taught us anything, it may be just how closely we are all connected. A book by Susan Hekman I reviewed several years ago, *Private Selves, Public Identities*, now, from a distance, issues a thought-provoking idea that I am compelled to take up here—namely, that the self-discoveries we are talking about when reflecting on musical awakenings such as those discussed above, critically important as they are, are indeed only one side of the story. What continue to be at play are also the public, collective identities we inherit and form in association with others. Does music, including classical music, have anything to do with such identities? And with the projection of self-discovery, indefinable as it may be, into our social lives?

I believe it does. It certainly did in the past. Many examples can be given of a classical music that played a sure role in fostering those intellectual and sentimental/emotional dimensions of private individuals, but which also, in a sort of twofold process, fostered senses of collective identity in the theaters and salons. Think respectively of Verdi's operas and Chopin's Mazurkas. In quite different ways, these works, and their artistic worlds, were even involved in processes of nation-building—processes that at the same time exceeded strictly singular national dimensions.

Is it still possible to broaden the horizon, to move beyond an understanding of classical music as a niche genre addressed to one's circle or even one's family or merely oneself? The question takes on special urgency under the condition of "social distancing," i.e. isolation, during the pandemic—an unforeseen condition in which music is no longer shared in a public venue, but negotiated through technology.

I take the basis for an answer from Giuseppe Mazzini's *Filosofia della musica*. Mazzini (1805–1872) was an Italian revolutionary, politician, and philosopher that one is not inclined to link with writings or thoughts about music. But this *Philosophy of Music* was his first book after a serious crisis, during which he was imprisoned and close friends died after being tortured as political prisoners (they were listed as "suicides"). Mazzini began by acknowledging that he was no musician, while stating at the same time that music was fundamental. He understood that, through the publication of his pamphlets while in exile, he could have influenced only a few intellectuals; but it was through music that a message could reach almost everyone, by way of different, and not merely intellectual, means. I should stress that he published that book in 1836, conveying an extremely strong criticism of the music that, with some exceptions, was still being created and propagated following a Rossinian tradition that Mazzini abhorred, precisely because it was rooted in what he saw as individualism and materialism. But he also saw the seeds of something new and better in works by Donizetti and Bellini. These seeds would be taken up by a rising star who at the time had not yet written *Nabucco* (1842), an opera that seems to incorporate to the letter more than one of the practical musical recommendations with which Mazzini's essay ends—recurrent motifs, active use of the chorus to represent a popular feeling, accompanied recitative, and historically grounded plots in which audiences could clearly identify, and identify with, positions of power and social relationships.

Let me conclude by recalling a few questions Mazzini posed to his contemporaries and still poses to us today. They all follow from a first question that I deem central for both composers and performers: "Which way should the genius walk?" but even more importantly, "To which problem should we seek a solution?" (Mazzini, 1943: 130, my translation). What intrigues me about the thoughts that follow from these originating questions, which precipitate in turn many other questions, is that Mazzini's preoccupation is always plural. Or better: it is an interplay between the singular and the plural. And are we not determined precisely by this matter of one and many?

> [Artistic possibilities and] tendencies are nearly infinite, just like the minds that create them. But all of them, if we consider them carefully by looking at the substance and concept and soul of the music, and not just secondary questions of forms and various other accessories, can basically be reduced to two. All of them, though preserving their different ranks, can be ordered into two great series, concentrating around two capital elements. These are the elements of all things: the two principles that operate continuously, and appear—at times the one prevails, other times the other—in all the problems that, throughout the ages, trouble the human intellect: two terms that emerge in all the struggles, and whose progressive development through two converging lines, century after century, form the matter of history. They are man and humanity—the individual thought and the social thought (Mazzini, 1943: 130–1).

Mazzini translates these two first principles into musical terms as melody and harmony. In that way he identified the ganglia of the question, giving us still— I believe—food for thought, no matter how we may prefer to put things in different musical-theoretical terms. (None other than Schoenberg insisted on this very "reciprocation between melody and harmony," which first reached a "perfect unity" in his *Kammersymphonie*, Op. 9) (Schoenberg, 1949).[1] The relationship between the individual and social thought, as reflected in the

---

[1] See also, Schoenberg 1952.

relationship between melody and harmony, has something sacred to it from a Mazzinian perspective: "In the perfect accord of these two terms, fundamental to any music—and then, in the consecration of this accord towards a sublime aim, a holy mission—lies the secret of the Art, the concept indeed of that European music that we all, consciously or unconsciously, invoke" (Mazzini, 1943: 132). In my view, it is the combination of these two dimensions, the individual and the social, that is still crucial in our troubled world, perhaps more than ever in the hyperconnected world we live in. If music—classical music first and foremost—reflects these dimensions, then it may also entail or promise some sort of social as well as individual awakening.

References

Hekman, S. 2004. *Private Selves, Public Identities: Reconsidering Identity Politics.* University Park, PA: Penn State University Press.

Glasgow, E. 1925. *Barren Ground.* Project Gutenberg Australia, http://gutenberg.net.au/ebooks07/0700091h.html. Accessed February 26, 2021.

Mazzini, G. 1943. *Filosofia della musica.* Milano: Fratelli Bocca, 1943.

Oxford Lieder. 2021. "L'indifferent." https://www.oxfordlieder.co.uk/song/4539. Accessed February 26, 2021.

Schoenberg, A. 1949. "My Evolution." Lecture delivered at the University of California at Los Angeles, Nov. 2, 1949. https://schoenberg.at/index.php/en/archiv-2/schoenberg-spricht?id=965:vr01. Accessed February 28, 2021.

--------.1952. "My Evolution." *Musical Quarterly* 38: 517-527.

Wang, A. "Five Minutes that Will Make You Love Classical Music." *The New York Times*, Sept. 6, 2018. https://www.nytimes.com/2018/09/06/arts/music/5-minutes-that-will-make-you-love-classical-music.html. Accessed February 26, 2021.

Authors and Performers

Animo, flute and piano duo, is formed by Sarah Waycott, flautist, and Yanna Zissiadou, pianist. Sarah is a UK-based versatile flautist, cellist, conductor, and music teacher with experience in performing a wide range of musical styles. A graduate of Bath Spa University and the Royal Welsh College of Music and Drama, Sarah has performed for Royalty and in venues across the UK and abroad. Described as "a fine flautist" by Roberto Bigio in the British Flute Society Journal, Sarah is a champion of new music as well as the standard flute repertoire. Animo is Sarah's most recent venture, which captures her style and diversity, particularly in Animo's first EP "Animo one." Yanna was born in Thessaloniki, Greece, and has lived in the UK for over 27 years. After graduating from the Royal Academy of Music in London and the Eastman School of Music in the U.S.A., Yanna developed her professional career as a concert pianist, chamber musician, accompanist, conductor, educator, and musical director. Having retired from classroom music teaching in 2016, Yanna joined Sarah in forming Animo while also fulfilling a long-term ambition to showcase Greek music for solo piano. Yanna and Sarah have the same approach to making music: to play soulful music free of labels. animofluteandpiano@gmail.com

Arquia Duo. The Arquia Duo members—Lisa Archontidi-Tsaldaraki, violin, and Tiffany Qiu, piano—are currently studying at the Royal Academy of Music (Lisa in the class of Rodney Friend and Tiffany in the class of Iain Fountain). Both have won many national and international awards, and have performed in well-known venues such as the Royal Albert Hall (Lisa as both member of NYO GB and leader of BYCO youth orchestra) and Carnegie Hall (Tiffany as soloist with the New York Sinfonietta). They formed the Arquia Duo in late 2019, and share a keen interest in contemporary classical music. elissavet.archonti19@ram.ac.uk, tiffany.qiu19@ram.ac.uk

Francisco Castillo works in the musicology department of the FJdC District University – ASAB in Bogotá. He has been academic editor of several books on historiography, music analysis, and education, and has published articles on musical perception and medieval notation. In addition to his work teaching music history, his research focuses on the historiography of Western music and music education. He is also a performer of early music on both the harpsichord and the baroque traverso flute. fjcastillog@udistrital.edu.co

The Eurasia Quartet recently won first prize at the second AEMC International Chamber Music Competition, and the quartet's appearance in this publication is part of that prize. The quartet was founded in Maastricht, The Netherlands, in 2013, and is named after the fact that each of its members has a strong connection to Russia, a country that combines European and Asian musical traditions. The Quartet is formed by Asia Czaj (violin), Egle Kaunietyte (violin), Ekaterina Degtiareva (viola), and Stanislav Degtyarev (cello). info@eurasiaquartet.nl

Dúo Francés-Bernal. Daniel Francés is a Spanish born violinist focused on chamber music playing. His recordings include projects with: "Flamenco contemporáneo Ensemble" and "Hispania Ensemble," in collaboration with pianist and composer Miguel A. Remiro; "Joyas recuperadas," with the Salduie piano trio; and "String delights," with the Gala string quartet and string trio. Since 2014 Daniel has worked closely with Sergio Bernal. Pianist Sergio Bernal is an active soloist, chamber musician, and Lied and opera accompanist. Also a member of Manebae Piano Duo, Sergio is very active in the field of chamber music. He is author and co-author of books and articles in journals on music and education, and is dedicated to piano and chamber music teaching in several conservatories. He is currently professor at the Conservatorio Superior de Música de Aragón (Spain). The Duo specializes in Spanish classical music, and has been invited to perform in several chamber music festivals in Spain and Europe. duofrancesbernal@gmail.com

Özgecan Karadağlı received her PhD in Music from the University of Alberta in 2017. An interdisciplinary researcher, she specializes in music and nationalism, Western art music in the Ottoman Empire, Riemannian and Neo-Riemannian theories, and the history of music theory. Her dissertation, *From Empire to Republic: Western Art Music, Nationalism, and the Merging Mediation of Saygun's Op. 26 Yunus Emre Oratorio*, focuses on Western art music during the nineteenth-century Ottoman Empire and the early Republic of Turkey in the construction of a national identity and of cultural politics. She has taught aural and keyboard skills and music theory at the University of Alberta. ozgecan.karadagli@gmail.com

Lawrence Kramer is Distinguished Professor of English and Music at Fordham University. He is the author of fourteen books on music, most recently the trilogy *Interpreting Music, Expression and Truth*, and *The Thought of Music*, winner of the 2017 ASCAP Foundation Virgil Thomson Award for Outstanding Music Criticism (University of California Press, 2010, 2012, 2016), plus *The Hum* *of the World: A Philosophy of Listening* (California, 2019). His work has been translated into nine languages and been the subject of scholarly meetings in the Americas, Europe, and China. His music, including eight string quartets and fifteen song cycles, has been performed throughout the United States and Europe. lkramer@fordham.edu

Amy Damron Kyle is a third-year musicology doctoral student at the Sorbonne University in Paris. Through historical and theoretical analyses of three operettas of Pauline Viardot-Garcia (notably including the newly discovered operetta, *Partie de Whist*) her thesis investigates women composers' systematic exclusion from the musical canon during the nineteenth century. Amy previously taught music theory at both the University of Utah and Roxbury College in Boston. She presented a TEDx talk on women at the Sorbonne in October 2019, and speaks regularly in various conferences about the historical importance of great female composers. aldkyle@gmail.com

Federica Marsico is a Marie Curie researcher at Ca' Foscari University of Venice and at McGill University of Montréal, where she conducts a three-year project entitled "Sexual and Gender Non-Normativity in Opera after the Second World War." She also lectures on the History of Music, the Musical Bibliography, and the History of Musical Theory at the Conservatory of Music of Cremona. Her research focuses on music theater between the nineteenth and twenty-first centuries. The author of several contributions to collective works and musicological journals, she has presented her research findings at numerous international conferences. She received a degree in piano performance in 2014, and a Ph.D. in Musicology in 2016. federica.marsico@unive.it

Alberto Nones is Professor of History and Aesthetics of Music at the "G. Puccini" Conservatory of Music of Gallarate, Italy, where he is also in charge of the artistic and didactic programming, with responsibility for the internationalization strategy. He is the author of four books on topics as diverse as Verdi, twentieth-century Italian opera composer Riccardo Zandonai, baroque composer Francesco Antonio Bonporti, and the Doors, and has published two edited volumes (one of which with Vernon Press) and articles in academic journals. A concert pianist, he has also recorded four CDs, including an acclaimed recording of the Complete Mazurkas by Chopin (Continuo Records, 2016). Since 2011, he has worked as an author and broadcaster of radio programs for RAI, the Italian national broadcast company. Professor Nones is the founder and president of the Associazione Europea di Musica e Comunicazione (AEMC), which organizes, among other things, an academic conference on "Music,

Communication, and Performance" that has caught the attention of scholars and musicians from all corners of the world. aemc.montecassiano@gmail.com

Hamish Robb is Senior Lecturer in Music Studies at Victoria University of Wellington, New Zealand. His research, teaching, and public engagement activities are informed by his triple expertise as musicologist, music theorist, and pianist. He earned his PhD from Princeton University, and his work has been published in journals including *Music Theory Online*, *Music Theory Spectrum*, and *Dance Research*. His research interests center on musical embodiment, performance studies, film music, piano pedagogy, and the music and theories of Marie Jaëll. hamish.robb@vuw.ac.nz

Deborah Stokol taught secondary school English and Journalism for 12 years (most recently at Brentwood School) after working as a reporter for several years before that. She currently lives in Los Angeles and is a composer, singer, pianist, Celtic harp-player, and beginning guitar- and mandolin-player. She recently released her debut album, "The Ill-Tempered Clavier" (Deborah Stokol, 2020) and a series of singles, all of which can be found on major platforms. dstokol@gmail.com

Trio Aperto was established in 2014 in Olomouc, in the Czech Republic. The ensemble focuses on Czech contemporary composers, mostly on music of the latter half of the twentieth century. The Trio's repertoire derives from the research of the oboist, Barbora Šteflová, who compiled a catalog of Czech contemporary works. The performances of this ensemble are currently being recorded by Czech Radio. The ensemble initiates new pieces from Czech composers, and promotes Czech contemporary music at festivals, such as Concentus Moraviae, Festival Forfest Czech Republic, The Harriet Parish Festival, L'Altra Stagione of Porto Recanati (Italy), and Meeting of New Music+. In 2019, the ensemble won third prize (ex-aequo) in the AEMC international chamber music competition. The Trio is composed by Barbora Šteflová, oboe, Pavel Horák, bassoon, and Jan Charfreitag, clarinet, who all play in national orchestras in the Czech Republic. Barbora.steflova@seznam.cz

Natalie Tsaldarakis is a researcher, pianist, and member of the Ivory Duo Piano Ensemble. She has recently published a review for the North American British Music Studies Association, and was the convenor of a public debate on the same topic as discussed in the present paper at City, University of London (June 2020). Natalie is pursuing doctoral studies, focusing on European pianistic traditions, under the supervision of Ian Pace. She is a trustee of the Cornelius Cardew Concerts Trust, has performed in venues such as Southbank and St-Martin-in-the-Fields, and has recently been signed by Convivium Records UK. ntsaldaraki@yahoo.com

AEMC Scientific Committee

Professor Alberto Nones, "G. Puccini" Conservatory of Music of Gallarate, President of AEMC

Professor Monika Fink, University of Innsbruck

Distinguished Professor Lawrence Kramer, Fordham University

Dr. Michael Maul, Bach-Archiv Leipig

Professor Letizia Michielon, "B. Marcello" Conservatory of Music of Venezia

Dr. Hamish Robb, Victoria University of Wellington

Notes on the Pieces that Appear in the Enclosed CD[1]

Animo perform Lukas Piel: *The Journey of Alan Kurdi*

In 2019 we commissioned Lukas Piel, a German composer and sound designer, to write a piece for Animo with the brief to produce a score for live acoustic instruments against a pre-recorded electronic soundscape backdrop. All our commissions are, in some degree, collaborations between the composer and us, but Lukas's idea for this work captured our imagination from the first draft and had a profound effect on us as performers. It is also shaping our "declassified" status even further. The Journey of Alan Kurdi received its online premiere during the third AEMC Conference in June 2020, and its live premiere at our "Jailbreak" concert in August 2020. The piece is based on 3-year-old Aylan Shenu's (Alan Kurdi's) tragic death from drowning when he and his family tried to escape war-torn Syria for a better life in another country. The image of Aylan's washed-up little body on a Turkish beach rocketed across the globe and brought hearts and minds together and, sadly, only a short-lived promise to give refuge to those in need. Lukas's intention is to remind us of our own humanity. The pulsing percussion, ethnic virtual instruments interlaced with acoustic timbres, vocalisms against crushing drum punctuations, shimmering shakers, and distant high pitch sustained notes create a mesmerizing and powerful soundscape backdrop that supports the flute and piano's storytelling. In Lukas's words, "The running out of time is presented by the constant ticking of the clock and is a central element to the piece." There is a constant pulse of electronic, virtual, manipulated sounds that interlock to create new instrumental timbres. We are quickly immersed in his timbral landscape, and enter the story through a visceral connection to Lukas's sound matrix. The piano and flute enter in turn, and the story unfolds without haste, following the unrelenting passage of time and Aylan's tragic death as time and waves continue to beat next to him. Even the simple clock ticking rhythm is a complex blend of smaller rhythmic impulses. Small motifs become bigger sound gestures, and capsizing emotions envelop the simpler flute and piano dialog. Lukas's composition is both epic and introspective, and encapsulates a much bigger human story in seven minutes and six seconds.

---

[1] The audio CD is available with the hardback version of this title only, ISBN: 978-1-64889-213-4. The audio tracks can be downloaded at: https://vernonpress.com/book/1281

"Animo Declassified" is our essence: we embrace and amalgamate styles to stir emotion, ask universal questions, move boundaries. Music can speak for itself, without labels.

Animo, flute and piano duo

Eurasia Quartet performs Lawrence Kramer: String Quartet No. 8, *Reflections and Memories*

The title Reflections and Memories describes the alternating states of mind from which this quartet is built, one thoughtful and searching, the other vivid and immediate. The music imagines these states neither as opposites nor as parallels, but as complements that call for and complete each other: thought seeking its sensory form and sensation seeking its place in thought. The four movements—Reflection I, "Mackerel Sky," Reflection II, and "Clouds. Wind. Stars"—follow the quasi-Baroque pattern slow-fast-slow-fast, suggesting a cyclical process rather than a narrative progression. But the cycle is nonetheless shaped by changes of attitude, in a crisscross pattern: the second slow movement is more troubled than the first, while the first fast movement is more troubled than the second.

The memories, by the way, are real ones, of cloud formations with strong personal associations. The memory movements trace the flow of such associations—it doesn't matter what they are—while the Reflections trace their inner reverberations. Each of the four movements features an element of texture or melody that becomes its unique signature; the four movements are linked by a kind of quickening or pulsation that recurs throughout in different forms.

Reflections and Memories, splendidly performed here by the Eurasia quartet, is about 21 minutes long. Its first three movements were composed in 2018 and 2020; the finale was composed as an independent piece in 2013 (it was the winner of the first Composers Concordance "Generations" prize), and may still be played on its own.

Lawrence Kramer

Duo Bernal-Francés performs Turina's *Variaciones clásicas*: the influence of traditional music in the creation of classical music

Joaquín Turina's life and work show an intimate contact with Spanish music and a personal attachment to its traditions. In 1929, the composer described how Andalusian folk music (both popular song and dance rhythm) had entered fully into Spanish music, becoming the core of symphonic works, "not only of the poem or the impression, but also of the classical forms, the sonata and others, symphony and chamber music." Turina pointed out three possibilities in the incorporation of folk material into music: literal transcription, "as a transplant"; the invention-imitation of popular formulas; and "the soul and the feeling of a Spanish region throbbing into music." The latter, he professed, "is the most difficult, but also the most beautiful form of expression." The composer must write his own folk material because the melodic line means little by itself "if it is not submerged, so to speak, in the air, in the light, in the fragrance of the region, shaping an unmistakable profile." Assimilation rather than reproduction, a folklore imaginaire (S. Moreux), a creation which is capable of evocation. The search for this evocation (a recurring word in the composer's writings) is a key aspect in the reception of his music, which fosters recognition of the content and the musical meaning of his work.

Variaciones Clásicas is "almost a fantasy," with tonal and modal tensions, ternary and binary rhythms, syncopations, off-beats accents, the "Andalusian triplet," vocal expressiveness, and guitar plucking, or the flamenco dance's taconeo. Its motifs reappear throughout the piece, intertwined with another pulse, tempo, and/or character. Turina described the piece in El canto andaluz en el arte de la música (1936): "A main theme, almost a sad regret, takes on different aspects, according to the work's development. The first variation moves with a lazy swing that sounds like a guajira in feeling although it does not carry the same combination of bars as the typical Cuban song. In the second variation, we hear, in the distance, a couplet of seguidillas. The third variation is a tango, very rhythmic, that prepares the fourth one, a melodic evocation of very light sonority, sung by the muted violin. The end is cheerful and fast, recalling the zapateado rhythm." Turina used this musical folklore to vary the theme, build the different episodes, and elaborate the form. This modus operandi can also be heard in previous works, e.g. the Piano Trio Op. 35 (Thème et Variations), where a muñeira, a schottis, a zortzico, a jota, and a soleá are present. The identity and strong evocative charge of Spanish popular song and dance, a prominent feature in Turina's work, contain meaningful elements that the listener is able to recognize, incorporate, or even assume as his own. This folklore imaginaire comes from a living tradition, and it can become part of the collective memory. This is what makes music last.

Duo Francés-Bernal

Deborah Stokol, "The Classics are Alive: Teaching the Bardic Tradition as a Bard"

Homer's *The Odyssey* and *The Iliad* embody the bardic tradition. I am a teacher who uses the bardic tools of voice and harp to perform extracts from these works in their original medium in order to make them come alive for my students. This also enables the students to grasp why such literature still matters—the way classical music still matters—how they can take ownership of it in creative ways, and why both the words and the music concern what it means to grapple with our mortality, that is, what it means to be human. Recorded and produced at home by Deborah Stokol, 2020.

Deborah Stokol

Arquia Duo performs C. Debussy: Sonata for Violin and Piano L.140

The Sonata in G Minor for Violin and Piano, L.140, was written in 1917 while Debussy suffered from cancer which eventually claimed his life in 1918. Premiered with violinist Gaston Poulet and the composer at the piano, this rather brief sonata has three movements (Allegro Vivo, Intermède: Fantasque et Léger, Finale: Très Animé). It was conceived as part of a cycle of six sonatas for various instruments, in homage to eighteenth-century French composers, especially Couperin and Rameau, by a composer weary of the darkness of raging war. Recorded live at the Henry Wood Room, Royal Academy of Music (UK).

Arquia Duo

Trio Aperto performs Pavel Kopecký: *Ritorni*

Pavel Kopecký (1949–) studied piano and cello before graduating from an Electro-Technical Secondary School and starting work with the sound department of Czech TV. He later studied composition, piano, and music pedagogy at the Academy of Performing Arts in Prague, and in summer courses in Siena, Italy with Franco Donatoni. Upon graduation he was granted a post-graduate scholarship to the Moscow State Conservatory to work with Nikolai Sidelnikov. His pieces were awarded competition prizes in 1973 and 1982 (the Valentino Bucchi Prize). Kopecký focuses on electroacoustic music. He has composed concert pieces such as *Reverberation* for cello and electroacoustics and *Diary of a Madman*, a piano suite based on a story by Nikolai Gogol, together with ballets such as *Luci serene* and various vocal pieces and film scores. Kopecký teaches in both the Department of Music and Sound and the Film and TV School at the Academy of Performing Arts in Prague as well as at the Jaroslav Ježek Jazz Conservatory. *Ritorni* is from 1989. This concert piece for wind trio and electroacoustic sounds lasts 10 minutes. It has a classical structure and consists of three parts: Praeludium, Passacaglia with gradation, and Postludium. The parts are connected with a short bassoon cadenza and a longer clarinet cadenza. The work employs two types of electro-acoustic sounds. The first consists of three music blocks, which derive from the sounds of the acoustic instruments. These are transformed, not just in terms of timbre, but of dynamics as well. In order to maintain the sonic integrity of the piece, the composer avoided using electronically generated sounds. The second type of electro-acoustic sound comes from real-time acoustic sounds of the instruments, which are miked and modified by two types of effects, namely delay and reverb. Their intensity and range change throughout the piece as managed by the sound engineer. *Ritorni* was recorded by the Novákovo Trio in 1999. The conference recording by Trio Aperto emerged from the Prague Festival Days of Contemporary Music held at The Academy of Performing Arts in Prague in 2019.

Trio Aperto

Track list

No.	Track's name	Duration	Performer
1.	L. Piel (1989–), *The Journey of Alan Kurdi* (2019)	7:06	**Animo**
	L. Kramer (1946–), String Quartet no. 8 *Reflections and Memories* (2018–2020)		**Eurasia Quartet**
2.	- Reflection I	4:12	**Eurasia Quartet**
3.	- Mackerel Sky	4:23	**Eurasia Quartet**
4.	- Reflection II	5:25	**Eurasia Quartet**
5.	- Clouds, Wind, Stars	6:17	**Eurasia Quartet**
6.	J. Turina (1882–1949), *Variaciones Clásicas* (1929)	11:17	**Duo Francés-Bernal**
7.	D. Stokol (1983–), Live Online Conference Presentation and Performance - *I am Odysseus* (2018–2020, D. Stokol translating Homer's *The Odyssey*) - *Song of Achilles: I'll Never See My Home, But My Name Shall Live Forever* (2018–2020, D. Stokol translating Homer's *The Iliad*) - *Ulysses* (2013, D. Stokol to the last stanza of Alfred Tennyson's "Ulysses")	5:53	**Deborah Stokol**
	C. Debussy (1862–1918), *Sonata for Violin and Piano* (1917)		**Arquia Duo**
8.	I Allegro vivo	4:54	**Arquia Duo**
9.	II Intermède: Fantasque et léger	4:09	**Arquia Duo**
10.	III Finale: Très animé	4:30	**Arquia Duo**
11.	P. Kopecký (1949–), *Ritorni* (1989)	10:21	**Trio Aperto**
	Total time: 68:42		

Index